Effective Practices for Teaching and Learning in Inclusive Classrooms

Revised First Edition

By Roberta Kaufman and Robert Wandberg

cognella
academic publishing

Bassim Hamadeh, CEO and Publisher
Michael Simpson, Vice President of Acquisitions
Jamie Giganti, Managing Editor
Jess Busch, Senior Graphic Designer
John Remington, Acquisitions Editor
Brian Fahey, Licensing Associate
Mandy Licata, Interior Designer

First published in the United States of America in 2014 by Cognella, Inc.

Printed in the United States of America

ISBN: 978-1-62661-888-6 (pbk) / 978-1-62661-889-3 (br)

www.cognella.com   800-200-3908

Contents

Chapter one

SETTING THE STAGE FOR LEARNING

All of us do not have equal talent but all of us should have an equal opportunity to develop our talent.

—PRESIDENT JOHN F. KENNEDY

OBJECTIVES

Readers will be able to:

1. Describe the makeup of the 21st-century classroom.

2. Discuss roles and responsibilities of the special education teacher in today's general education classroom.

3. Discuss roles and responsibilities of the general education teacher in today's classroom.

4. Identify terms, acronyms, and legal expectations associated with diverse student populations.

KEY VOCABULARY

Readers will be able to define or describe each term in the context of the chapter information.

Accommodations	Least Restrictive Environment	High-Impact Practices
Related Services	Individual Education Program	Special Education

INTRODUCTION

Achmed is a first grader who is easily distracted. He is taller than the rest of the first graders, speaks with a noticeable accent, and is constantly on the move. Academically, he is not progressing at a reasonable rate.

Mona is seven and a first grader. She is a child with a hearing impairment. Recently, she has engaged in more aggressive behavior toward peers, both on the playground and in the classroom, including bumping into and tripping others and pulling hair.

Joey and his mom have moved around a lot. He is a quiet student with few friends, but is a student who is making progress in all content areas. This success is in spite of the many absences documented for Joey.

All of the above children, along with many other diverse students, are in the classroom you are teaching. Each of their backgrounds and needs are very different. How will you handle these situations? Where do you start? Will your responses depend on your position as a general education teacher or a special education teacher? How will you make a difference in their academic achievement, while at the same time meeting the needs of all other students?

Who Are the Students in Today's General Education Classrooms?

It is a well-known fact that general education teachers are instructing a more diverse student population than their counterparts 20 years ago. The difference is that more students with challenging needs are being included in general education classes, not pulled out into specialized classrooms. Today, a typical classroom of 30 students may have as many as six students on an individualized education program (IEP), six others might be on a 504 plan, anywhere from zero to 80 percent may be English learners (EL), and still others have home situations that vary from normal to complex. High-achieving and gifted students are part of the mix as well. The range of intellect, ability, physical, social, emotional, and health-related needs in a single classroom is dramatic. For students with disabilities, the most recent statistics are found in Table 1.1.

Table 1.1 Fast Facts

Percentage distribution of students 6 to 21 years old served under Individuals with Disabilities Education Act, Part B, by educational environment and type of disability: Fall 2009

TYPE OF DISABILITY	ALL ENVIRONMENTS	REGULAR SCHOOL, TIME OUTSIDE GENERAL CLASS			SEPARATE SCHOOL FOR STUDENTS WITH DISABILITIES	SEPARATE RESIDENTIAL FACILITY	PARENTALLY PLACED IN REGULAR PRIVATE SCHOOLS	HOMEBOUND/ HOSPITAL PLACEMENT	CORRECTIONAL FACILITY
		LESS THAN 21 PERCENT	21–60 PERCENT	MORE THAN 60 PERCENT					
All students with disabilities	100.0	59.4	20.7	14.6	3.0[1]	0.4[1]	1.2[2]	0.4	0.4
Autism	100.0	37.4	18.3	34.8	8.0[1]	0.6[1]	0.7[2]	0.3	#
Deaf-blindness	100.0	21.6	13.3	33.3	19.1[1]	9.9[1]	0.6[2]	2.3	0.2
Developmental delay	100.0	61.6	20.5	16.2	0.9[1]	0.1[1]	0.6[2]	0.2	#
Emotional disturbance	100.0	40.6	18.8	22.2	13.2[1]	2.0[1]	0.2[2]	1.1	2.0
Hearing impairments	100.0	54.6	17.0	14.7	8.2[1]	4.0[1]	1.3[2]	0.2	0.1
Intellectual disability	100.0	17.4	26.7	48.2	6.3[1]	0.4[1]	0.3[2]	0.5	0.3
Multiple disabilities	100.0	13.2	16.2	45.5	19.6[1]	1.9[1]	0.4[2]	2.9	0.2
Orthopedic impairments	100.0	52.2	16.3	23.6	5.1[1]	0.2[1]	0.9[2]	1.7	0.1
Other health impairments[3]	100.0	61.4	23.8	10.8	1.6[1]	0.2[1]	1.1[2]	0.9	0.3
Specific learning disabilities	100.0	63.3	26.6	8.0	0.6[1]	0.1[1]	0.9[2]	0.2	0.4
Speech or language impairments	100.0	86.3	5.6	4.6	0.3[1]	#[1]	3.1[2]	0.1	#
Traumatic brain injury	100.0	46.4	23.8	21.5	5.2[1]	0.6[1]	0.7[2]	1.7	0.2
Visual impairments	100.0	62.6	13.5	12.0	6.2[1]	3.6[1]	1.4[2]	0.7	#

Rounds to zero.

SOURCE: U.S. Department of Education, National Center for Education Statistics (2012). *Digest of Education Statistics, 2011* (NCES 2012–001), Chapter 2.

1 Data for 2006 and later years combine public and private schools and combine public and private residential facilities.

2 Students who are enrolled by their parents or guardians in regular private schools and have their basic education paid through private resources, but receive special education services at public expense. These students are not included under "Regular school, time outside general class."

3 Other health impairments include having limited strength, vitality, or alertness due to chronic or acute health problems such as a heart condition, tuberculosis, rheumatic fever, nephritis, asthma, sickle cell anemia, hemophilia, epilepsy, lead poisoning, leukemia, or diabetes.

NOTE: Data are for the 50 United States, the District of Columbia, and the Bureau of Indian Education schools. Detail may not sum to totals because of rounding.

Case Studies: Diverse Students

The following diverse students with unique characteristics are found in an inclusive classroom.

STUDENT	CHARACTERISTICS
1. Achmed	Achmed is a first grader. He is easily distracted and not progressing academically when compared with his peers. He is a language learner.
2. Mona	Mona is seven and in the first grade. She has a hearing impairment. Mona is beginning to act out and become more aggressive with her peers.
3. Joey	Joey is in the fifth grade and has been absent a lot. Despite his absences, he is making academic progress. He is extremely quiet and has few friends.
4. Reid	Reid is a middle school student. He is fearful of speaking in front of his classmates. When asked to give oral reports and presentations he freezes.
5. Alejandra	Alejandra is in the seventh grade. She struggles with the English language. She becomes frustrated and gives up.
6. Blake	Blake is in the seventh grade. She has been identified as a gifted student.
7. Sarah	Sarah, a third grader, has childhood rheumatoid arthritis and uses a wheelchair to get around. She is on medication for a number of other medical issues and processes information slowly.
8. Tom	Tom is in the third grade. He is the class clown and generally devises a way to get out of completing class assignments. Tom is a slow methodological reader who forgets what he reads.

What Are the Challenges That Teachers Face in Today's Classrooms?

Educators in the 21st century recognize they must be trained not only in the discipline areas they are teaching, but also the nuances of the profession. Among the challenges for teachers is the ability to collaborate and communicate effectively with many other professionals and parents, differentiating instruction, organizing a classroom, establishing classroom routines and procedures, engaging students in instruction, assessing, grading, and documenting progress of students.

Each chapter in this book offers research-based practices to support today's teachers in very diverse classrooms. Whether you are going to be a general education teacher or a special educator in your own classroom or co-teaching, consistently using the instructional practices described in this text will promote academic achievement across multiple settings.

Learner Objectives

How will you know what to teach? Identifying objectives that address student needs and comply with standards associated with the content being taught can be difficult. Not only does a teacher need to create learner objectives, but also must be able to modify them according to the types of students in the classroom. Starting with a well-constructed learner objective focuses the direction of instruction. By knowing where you need to be at the end of a lesson, you will be able to assess the success of students in meeting the objective and modify if necessary.

Vocabulary

How can you teach so many different subjects using effective instruction? Teaching by way of using research-based practices challenges both novice and veteran teachers. Incorporating vocabulary instruction as a consistent instructional practice reinforces a student's knowledge base. Vocabulary presented in engaging ways becomes a means to student achievement. Linking academic vocabulary to lesson instruction promotes generalization of skills required in many content areas.

Visual Representations

Using visual representations across content areas is a high-impact practice in classrooms of diverse students. Sometimes called nonlinguistic representations, a visual is, as the adage says, worth a thousand words. Pictures, graphic organizers, and realia are all considered visuals that have a distinct place in the classroom, but there are many others. Just presenting a visual, however, is not the whole picture. Visuals must fit the learner outcome. Students who are able to construct visuals tend to become more independent learners.

Student Engagement

Many teachers confuse objectives with activities. Active learning engages students, but it does so purposefully. Engaging students requires thoughtful consideration of the learner outcomes. Differentiation is one of the keys to engaging diverse students in learning.

Grouping and Cooperative Learning

Managing classroom instruction and providing for the diverse needs of students involve the use of flexible grouping arrangements. Individualizing may mean there are times when a small group or cooperative learning is necessary. Deciding who is in the group, the size of the group, the function of the group or individual members of the group, and the longevity of the group are often questions teachers have. If you are in a classroom where co-teaching is practiced, is the pattern of grouping students effective?

Asking Questions

Teachers who develop the skill of asking questions incorporate multiple types of questions to involve and engage students. Questions that pose problems and promote critical thinking can be used across many content areas. Scaffolding questions based on a hierarchy of learning builds student confidence. Training students to use questions as they interact with text and content reinforces learning. A variety of question strategies that fit the purpose are helpful to have prepared.

Assessment and Grading

Assessment can and should take many forms. Differentiation in assessment allows students to show what they know in more than one way. Assessing students is an ongoing process used to plan instruction. Grading diverse students in a classroom may present teachers with some challenges, unless forethought has gone into designing the evaluative measure. Rubrics with clearly identified expectations provide consistency between teacher and student performance.

Why Are So Many Special Education Students in General Education Classrooms?

It is estimated that 95 percent of all students with disabilities are in general education classrooms (NCES, 2012). For many students on an IEP, the general education classroom is the least restrictive environment. Amazing as it may sound, the first special education teachers were often general education teachers who were requested by principals to take students with disabilities when the first law went into effect in 1975. In that regard, history is somewhat repeating itself.

Over time, multiple pathways were developed to train special education teachers. However, the need for special education teachers generally exceeded the rate of individuals graduating with a special education degree. The need for well-trained and qualified teachers in special education, in part, created an opportunity for more inclusive classrooms and co-teaching.

What Is the Role of the General Education Teacher in Today's Classroom?

The expertise of a classroom teacher is content. Whether it is language arts and reading or math and science, upper grades or primary classrooms, school boards hire teachers who are qualified to teach subject matter and manage classrooms full of students.

What Is the Role of the Special Education Teacher?

Special education teachers are experts in various disabilities, legal requirements associated with providing education and related services, and making curricular, instructional, or behavioral accommodations based on the students' needs.

There are many similarities between the role of the general education teacher and the role of education specialists, such as special education and English-language teachers. The Council of Chief State School Officers (CCSSO, 2011) offers a set of model core teaching standards that outline what teachers should know and be able to do to ensure every K–12 student reaches the goal of being ready to enter college or the workforce in today's world. These standards outline the common principles and foundations of teaching practice that cut across all subject areas and grade levels and that are necessary to improve student achievement. There are ten standards that have been grouped into four general categories.

Group 1: The Learner and Learning

Standard #1: Learner Development. The teacher understands how learners grow and develop, recognizing that patterns of learning and development vary individually within and across the cognitive, linguistic, social, emotional, and physical areas, and designs and implements developmentally appropriate and challenging learning experiences.

Standard #2: Learning Differences. The teacher uses understanding of individual differences and diverse cultures and communities to ensure inclusive learning environments that enable each learner to meet high standards.

Standard #3: Learning Environments. The teacher works with others to create environments that support individual and collaborative learning and that encourage positive social interaction, active engagement in learning, and self-motivation.

Group 2: Content

Standard #4: Content Knowledge. The teacher understands the central concepts, tools of inquiry, and structures of the discipline(s) he or she teaches and creates learning experiences that make the discipline accessible and meaningful for learners to assure mastery of the content.

Standard #5: Application of Content. The teacher understands how to connect concepts and use differing perspectives to engage learners in critical thinking, creativity, and collaborative problem solving related to authentic local and global issues.

Group 3: Instructional Practice

Standard #6: Assessment. The teacher understands and uses multiple methods of assessment to engage learners in their own growth, to monitor learner progress, and to guide the teacher's and learner's decision making.

Standard #7: Planning for Instruction. The teacher plans instruction that supports every student in meeting rigorous learning goals by drawing upon knowledge of content areas, curriculum, cross-disciplinary skills, and pedagogy, as well as knowledge of learners and the community context.

Standard #8: Instructional Strategies. The teacher understands and uses a variety of instructional strategies to encourage learners to develop deep understanding of content areas and their connections and to build skills to apply knowledge in meaningful ways.

Group 4: Professional Responsibility

Standard #9: Professional Learning and Ethical Practice. The teacher engages in ongoing professional learning and uses evidence to continually evaluate his or her practice, particularly the effects of his or her choices and actions on others (learners, families, other professionals, and the community) and adapts practice to meet the needs of each learner.

Standard #10: Leadership and Collaboration. The teacher seeks appropriate leadership roles and opportunities to take responsibility for student learning, to collaborate with learners, families, colleagues, other school professionals, and community members to ensure learner growth and to advance the profession.

These standards clearly indicate that teachers—of all subjects, all grades, and all learners—have a similar role. However, due to increased diversity in today's classroom, teachers have to work together and rely on each other's specific expertise to provide students with the most appropriate learning experiences possible.

How Do Background and Training Impact Work with Special Education Students?

In working with special education students, there has been a history of grandfathering teachers into the position and hiring individuals not fully prepared for the complex responsibilities. In addition, there are low numbers of graduates with special education majors and high turnover once in the profession. Most likely you will be a person who has come in through one of the six most common pathways into the field:

1. You have a bachelor's degree in a liberal arts content area with no experience or background in education, special education, or a related field.

2. You are fully licensed in some area of education, either an elementary degree or a secondary content area, not special education.

3. You are not licensed in any area of education, but considered a community expert based on experience in an associated field, such as years working as a mental health professional.

4. You are fully licensed in special education, not necessarily the category of disability or age level where you are working (e.g., autism; elementary license, but working in a secondary setting).

5. You are fully licensed in both special education and a secondary content area or elementary education.

6. You are a substitute or paraprofessional who may have an Associate's Degree (AA), but due to failure of all other attempts to hire a qualified licensed professional, a district responds by placing a temporary employee or hourly staff in the role of classroom teacher.

Identifying skills and knowledge can be helpful in reflecting on the level of confidence or need you may have when it comes to working with students with disabilities. Using Template 1.1: Pathway to Working with Diverse Students at the end of this chapter, rate your current knowledge and skills related to working with diverse students.

What Is the Role of Other Specialists in Today's General Education Classrooms?

The general education setting hosts many professionals during the school year. Working in tandem reinforces consistency across many areas. Other professionals can provide support and research-based recommendations related to instruction and services needed by students.

Besides the special education teachers, there are speech and language therapists, physical and occupational therapists, school psychologists, perhaps English Learner (EL) teachers, medical doctors, nurses, counselors, behavioral interventionists, social workers, human services or judicial representatives, and many other professionals who are involved in the child's life. Each of these professionals has a role with responsibilities and language of their own you will need to negotiate. Table 1.2 below identifies some of the more apparent duties aligned with general education and special education teachers. There are, however, many more that can be added to the list.

Table 1.2 Roles and Responsibilities of Classroom Professionals

PROFESSIONAL	ROLES AND RESPONSIBILITIES
General Education Teacher	Instructional Planning Pedagogy Classroom Management Content Knowledge Core Content State Standards
Special Education Teacher	Instructional Accommodations Pedagogy Classroom Management Knowledge of Disabilities Legal and Procedural Rights

Professionals bring unique skills and strengths to a general education classroom. Collaboration and communication are essential in school settings. When professionals partner as team members, the needs of a diverse student population can be better met in a learning environment. Use Template 1.2: Roles and Responsibilities of Classroom Professionals found at the end of this chapter to identify others who will team with you in working with diverse student populations throughout the year.

Who Are the Special Education Students in Today's Classroom?

General education teachers often confess they have little training and sometimes little enthusiasm for teaching students with a disability. The characteristics and behaviors of students with disabilities can be complex. Getting to know the student's background, academic needs and instructional practices proven to be effective are the first steps and set the stage for a successful year.

Categories of Disabilities

Thirteen categories of disabilities have been defined by federal law and in each state to address the educational needs of children and young people from ages three to 22.

State definitions may vary somewhat, but the following are taken directly from IDEA 2004 (Authority: 20 U.S.C. 1401(3); 1401(30)) section 300.8 Child With a Disability.

1. Autism Spectrum Disorder

Autism means a developmental disability significantly affecting verbal and nonverbal communication and social interaction, generally evident before age three, that adversely affects a child's educational performance. Other characteristics often associated with autism are engagement in repetitive activities and stereotyped movements, resistance to environmental change or change in daily routines, and unusual responses to sensory experiences. (ii) Autism does not apply if a child's educational performance is adversely affected primarily because the child has an emotional disturbance, as defined in paragraph (c)(4) of this section. (iii) A child who manifests the characteristics of autism after age three could be identified as having autism if the criteria in paragraph (c)(1)(i) of this section are satisfied.

2. Cognitive Impairments

(6) Mental retardation means significantly subaverage general intellectual functioning, existing concurrently with deficits in adaptive behavior and manifested during the developmental period, that adversely affects a child's educational performance.

3. Deaf

Deafness means a hearing impairment that is so severe that the child is impaired in processing linguistic information through hearing, with or without amplification that adversely affects a child's educational performance.

4. Deaf/Blind

Deaf-blindness means concomitant hearing and visual impairments, the combination of which causes such severe communication and other developmental and educational needs that they cannot be accommodated in special education programs solely for children with deafness or children with blindness.

5. Emotional and Behavior Disorders

(i) Emotional disturbance means a condition exhibiting one or more of the following characteristics over a long period of time and to a marked degree that adversely affects a child's educational performance:

(A) An inability to learn that cannot be explained by intellectual, sensory, or health factors.

(B) An inability to build or maintain satisfactory interpersonal relationships with peers and teachers.

(C) Inappropriate types of behavior or feelings under normal circumstances.

(D) A general pervasive mood of unhappiness or depression.

(E) A tendency to develop physical symptoms or fears associated with personal or school problems.

(ii) Emotional disturbance includes schizophrenia. The term does not apply to children who are socially maladjusted, unless it is determined that they have an emotional disturbance under paragraph (c)(4)(i) of this section.

6. Hearing Impairment

Hearing impairment means an impairment in hearing, whether permanent or fluctuating, that adversely affects a child's educational performance but that is not included under the definition of deafness in this section.

7. Multiple, Severe Disabilities

Multiple disabilities means concomitant impairments (such as mental retardation-blindness or mental retardation-orthopedic impairment), the combination of which causes such severe educational needs that they cannot be accommodated in special education programs solely for one of the impairments. Multiple disabilities does not include deaf-blindness.

8. Orthopedic Impairment

Orthopedic impairment means a severe orthopedic impairment that adversely affects a child's educational performance. The term includes impairments caused by a congenital anomaly, impairments caused by disease (e.g., poliomyelitis, bone tuberculosis), and impairments from other causes (e.g., cerebral palsy, amputations, and fractures or burns that cause contractures).

9. Other Health Impairments

Other health impairment means having limited strength, vitality, or alertness, including a heightened alertness to environmental stimuli, that results in limited alertness with respect to the educational environment, that—(i) Is due to chronic or acute health problems such as asthma, attention deficit disorder or attention deficit hyperactivity disorder, diabetes, epilepsy, a heart condition, hemophilia, lead poisoning, leukemia, nephritis, rheumatic fever, sickle cell anemia, and Tourette syndrome; and (ii) Adversely affects a child's educational performance.

10. Specific Learning Disabilities

(i) General. Specific learning disability means a disorder in one or more of the basic psychological processes involved in understanding or in using language, spoken or written, that may manifest itself in the imperfect ability to listen, think, speak, read, write, spell, or to do mathematical calculations, including conditions such as perceptual disabilities, brain injury, minimal brain dysfunction, dyslexia, and developmental aphasia.

(ii) Disorders not included. Specific learning disability does not include learning problems that are primarily the result of visual, hearing, or motor disabilities, of mental retardation, of emotional disturbance, or of environmental, cultural, or economic disadvantage.

11. Speech and Language Impairment

Speech or language impairment means a communication disorder, such as stuttering, impaired articulation, a language impairment, or a voice impairment, that adversely affects a child's educational performance.

12. Traumatic Brain Injury

Traumatic brain injury means an acquired injury to the brain caused by an external physical force, resulting in total or partial functional disability or psychosocial impairment, or both, that adversely affects a child's educational performance. Traumatic brain injury applies to open or closed head injuries resulting in impairments in one or more areas, such as cognition; language; memory; attention; reasoning; abstract thinking; judgment; problem-solving; sensory, perceptual, and motor abilities; psychosocial behavior; physical functions; information processing; and speech. Traumatic brain injury does not apply to brain injuries that are congenital or degenerative, or to brain injuries induced by birth trauma.

13. Visual Impairment and Blindness

Visual impairment including blindness means an impairment in vision that, even with correction, adversely affects a child's educational performance. The term includes both partial sight and blindness.

What Does the Law Say about Teaching Special Education Students in the General Education Classroom?

The law says education of students with disabilities should be in the least restrictive environment. The location of the student's education must be as close to their peers as possible and must include access to curriculum similar to students without disabilities. Any deviation from the general education classroom is accompanied by justification as to why another setting will be more beneficial to the students' education. Any placement is a team decision.

Placements can change over time. A student may need more intensive instruction or behavioral supports, which would require a more restrictive environment. Documented success in managing academic or social skills for an extended period of time can result in more inclusion with peers.

Just as a caveat, not all students with disabilities should be in a general education classroom a majority of the day or at all. There are many other placements and settings that may need to be considered, depending on the nature of the disability and needs of the child. Special education is a service—not a placement.

What Is Special Education, Exactly?

In short, special education, as defined by PL 94:142 in 1974, is specially designed instruction and related services, at no cost to parents, to meet the educational needs of students with disabilities. It is free, appropriate, public education that is provided in the least restrictive environment. Special education is based on multiple assessments given by a variety of professionals who are knowledgeable of the child and the disability. The due process rights of parents and the child, as well as teachers, are ensured.

Special education is designed to meet the academic needs of children and youth with disabilities. Learning is impacted not only by the disability, but the placement of a child in a setting, as well as economic, social-emotional, medical, and environmental factors. As in other aspects of public education, the special education pendulum kept swinging, and reforms were initiated. Over time, the federal government, in conversation with state governors, determined schools were ailing. High dropout rates, low graduation rates, poor performance by subsets of students (including students with disabilities), prompted more attention from education officials. The standards movement examined who was teaching students with disabilities, as well as how and what they were being taught.

What Is an Individualized Education Program?

You can sit in the teachers' lounge and listen to stories about children and families who may be part of the special education merry-go-round, but that is NOT recommended. As one of the team members engaged in the education of a child with a disability, a better plan is to study the individualized education program. An IEP is a legal document that identifies the needs, as well as the services, in place to benefit the student's education, including academic, behavior, social, and sometimes health-related concerns. The IEP creates a picture of the student's strengths and concerns, as well as the justification for a placement designed to access curriculum and general education peers to the extent possible. It tells who does what, when, and where. It provides accountability.

A closer examination and discussion of an IEP document creates a better understanding of the roles and responsibilities expected when working with students included in the general education classroom. Some districts implement a summary of the IEP as seen in Figure 1.1 below.

Figure 1.1 IEP at a Glance

Student:	Identification Number:
Grade:	Date:
Teacher(s):	Class:
Goals Linked to Common Core Standards: *(Specific to the class)*	
Instructional Accommodations:	
Assessment Accommodations:	
Accommodations to the Environment:	

The most recent changes to IEPs came in 2004, signed into law by President George W. Bush. The following are the changes highlighted by the Office of Special Education and Rehabilitative Services (OSERS) in the U.S. Department of Education and can be found at www.ideapartnership.org.

1. As used in Part 300, the term individualized education program or IEP means a written statement for each child with a disability that is developed, reviewed, and revised in a meeting in accordance with 34 CFR 300.320 through 300.324, and that must include:

    - A statement of the child's present levels of academic achievement and functional performance ...
    - A statement of measurable annual goals, including academic and functional goals designed to:
        o Meet the child's needs that result from the child's disability to enable the child to be involved in and make progress in the general education curriculum; and
        o Meet each of the child's other educational needs that result from the child's disability;
    - For children with disabilities who take alternate assessments aligned to alternate achievement standards, a description of benchmarks or short-term objectives;
    - A description of:
        o How the child's progress toward meeting the annual goals described in 34 CFR 300.320(a)(2) will be measured; and
        o When periodic reports on the progress the child is making toward meeting the annual goals (such as through the use of quarterly or other periodic reports, concurrent with the issuance of report cards) will be provided;
    - A statement of the special education and related services and supplementary aids and services, based on peer-reviewed research to the extent practicable, to be provided to the child, or on behalf of the child ...
    - A statement of any individual appropriate accommodations that are necessary to measure the academic achievement and functional performance of the child on State and district-wide assessments consistent with section 612(a)(16) of the Act; and if the IEP Team determines that the child must take an alternate assessment instead of a particular regular State or district-wide assessment of student achievement, a statement of why the child cannot participate in the regular assessment and why the particular alternate assessment selected is appropriate for the child. ... [34 CFR 300.320(a)] [20 U.S.C. 1414(d)(1)(A)(i)]

2. Revised requirements for the content of IEPs relating to transition services.

   Beginning not later than the first IEP to be in effect when the child turns 16, or younger if determined appropriate by the IEP Team, and updated annually thereafter, the IEP must include:

   - Appropriate measurable postsecondary goals based upon age-appropriate transition assessments related to training, education, employment, and, where appropriate, independent living skills; and
   - The transition services (including courses of study) needed to assist the child in reaching those goals. [34 CFR 300.320(b)] [20 U.S.C. 1414(d)(1)(A)(i)(VIII)(aa) and (bb)]

3. Clarify requirements regarding transfer of rights.

   Beginning not later than one year before the child reaches the age of majority under State law, the IEP must include a statement that the child has been informed of the child's rights under Part B of the Act, if any, that will transfer to the child on reaching the age of majority under 34 CFR 300.520. Authority: [34 CFR 300.320(c)] [20 U.S.C. 1414(d)(1)(A)(i)(VIII)(cc)]

How Do Teachers Decipher Legal Terms and Acronyms?

Much is made about the jargon of special education. Alphabet soup is common when it comes to how disabilities, programs, and services are discussed among the professionals who are accustomed to working with students having exceptional learning needs.

Here is a helpful list of ABC suggestions to get started on the acronym journey. The statements below identify different legal aspects of working with diverse student populations.

1. *Assessment* is necessary for diagnosis, placement, and instruction.

2. *(un)Biased* assessment involves multiple professionals engaged in the process of using multiple valid and reliable measures related to the concerns observed.

3. *Changes* in placement require team meetings, not arbitrary decisions.

4. *Due* process—The special education principle that provides legal recourse and timely resolution of disputes.

5. *Evidence-based* practices are those found to have a high impact on student achievement.

6. *Free* appropriate public education—This is one of the major principles of special education law.

7. *Generate* multiple solutions to solve a problem.

8. *Hearings,* arbitration and mediation are initiated prior to legal recourse in disputes.

9. *IEPs* at a glance are one-page summaries listing a child's goals and classroom accommodations, as well as other individualized services.

10. *Justification* of a student's placement in other than a general education setting is required.

11. *Keeping* accurate data assists with progress monitoring and reporting.

12. *Levels* of performance—The present level of performance identifies behavior and academic strengths or concerns of a student as a result of observations, assessments of curriculum, or normed procedures.

13. *Multidisciplinary* assessment—The special education principle requiring a variety of unbiased assessments in the child's native language as a diagnosis and determination of a disability and throughout the educational process.

14. *Needs* and strengths are included in the Present Level of Performance (PLOP).

15. *Organize* student data using visuals to discuss progress.

16. *Parents'* rights—The special education principle reinforcing the involvement of parents in every assessment, placement, and educational decisions.

17. *(re)Quest* training to learn more about assistive technology, a disability area, or other topics that will help you be a more effective teacher.

18. *Related* services are identified on an IEP as needed by students to benefit from education.

19. *Summer* school is not the same as an extended school year (ESY).

20. *Talented* and gifted students benefit from differentiation as much as EL and students on IEPs.

21. *Use* common core state standards to assist in writing annual goals.

22. *Voice* your ideas and concerns at team meetings.

23. *Written* notices of meetings are required and friendly reminders are helpful.

24. *(e)Xamine* data to make instructional decisions.

25. *Yearly* meetings are required to update the IEP.

26. *Zero* reject—The special education principle that no student with a disability is denied access to education.

Keeping a journal of alphabet soup special education terms is a recommended practice. Together with others involved in the instruction and life of the student on an IEP, it is wise to create a dictionary of acronyms that are used. Whether you are a general education teacher, a special education teacher, or other individual working with students with disabilities, you can increase communication across professionals and build understanding of roles and responsibilities by better understanding terminology. Use Template 1.5: An Acronym Journal at the end of the chapter to create a personalized list of terms and legal language.

How Do You Reach and Teach All Students in a General Education Classroom?

Teachers who are organized tend to have classrooms that lend themselves to diverse learners. The structure is predictable. Routines and rituals have been established. Students know what to expect. Teachers are intent on implementing instructional practices that promote differentiation in content, product, and processes in order to have a positive impact on student learning. A growing area of differentiation includes that of the concepts of Universal Design for Learning (UDL).

What Is the Difference between a Non-Differentiated and Differentiated Classroom?

In a classroom where the teacher does not employ the concept of differentiation, there is little preparation given to incorporating multiple materials for purposes of demonstration. Instruction may consist of teacher lecture and students taking notes or completing written assignments in lockstep fashion. The assessment of knowledge may be limited to tests and rarely take into account the variety of performance or product options that involve other styles of learning. In a non-differentiated classroom, accommodations for diverse students are not fluid or part of the planning process. Concrete and sequential may prevail over providing just the right challenge for many types of learners. In contrast, differentiation is a practice and philosophy that meets the needs of diverse learners, whether they be students with disabilities, academically at risk, unmotivated, gifted, socially awkward students, or English-language learners.

Differentiated instruction is characterized by the fact that three areas of instruction—content, process, and product—can be made flexible in ways to promote the success of every student. No single teaching method works for every learner. Universal Design for Learning supports differentiation and identifies three principles of learning. They are: recognition, strategic, and affective learning.

Principle 1: Recognition

A teacher who provides multiple content examples during instruction and many opportunities to interact with different types of content materials before, during, and after instruction sets the stage for diverse learners. This practice promotes the development of recognition and patterned thinking. It builds schema and both builds upon and builds prior knowledge for future learning.

Hall, Strangman, and Meyer (2011) give the following example of recognition: In a social studies class to help students understand where a state is located, a teacher would begin by showing an atlas or a globe, Googling a state map on the SmartBoard, or describing the state's location in words. Without changing the core content, the teacher could vary the difficulty of the material by presenting smaller or larger, simpler or more complex (such as topographical or physical) maps. For students with physical or intellectual disabilities, the variety of examples may be vital in order for them to access the pattern being taught. Other students may benefit from the same multiple examples by gaining a new a perspective.

In UDL, multiple content examples are reinforced by providing multiple media and formats. The wide range of digital tools available for digital presentations of instructional content allows teachers to manipulate size, color contrasts, volume, and other features, which can be saved and flexibly accessed in the future.

The teacher who maintains a focus on the learner objective and highlights critical features of content supports differentiated instruction. Hall, Strangman, and Meyer (2011) note that when teachers focus on essential components, limit the focus on extensive facts or extraneous details, and reiterate broad concepts or big picture ideas, one of the goals of differentiated instruction—that of reinforcing student recognition—is met. Finally, by assessing and supporting background knowledge, a teacher can better scaffold instruction as part of the differentiation process.

Principle 2: Strategic Learning

Teachers who vary teaching methods recognize that flexibility is important to help meet the needs of their diverse students who have very different learning strategies and styles. Differentiated instruction, as noted previously, uses the practice of demonstrating information and skills multiple times and at varying levels, which encourages diverse learners to engage with the material. When students are engaged in initial learning on novel tasks or skills, scaffolding and supported practice ensures success and eventual independence.

Supported practice enables students the opportunity to master a complex skill by dividing it into manageable parts. Differentiated instruction promotes this teaching method by encouraging students to be active and responsible learners and by asking teachers to respect individual differences and scaffold students as they move from initial learning to practiced, less-supported skills mastery (Hall, Strangman, & Meyer, 2011). Students are given flexible opportunities to demonstrate what they have learned. Differentiation allows a variety of assessment opportunities. Teachers can vary requirements and expectations for learning and expressing knowledge, as well as the degree of difficulty and the methods of grading.

Principle 3: Affective Learning

Both differentiated instruction and UDL recognize the importance of engaging learners in instructional tasks. Differentiated instruction includes effective classroom management and effective organizational and instructional practices. Teachers who differentiate offer choices in materials, adjust the level of difficulty, provide scaffolds, and integrate active learning throughout instruction to maintain learner attention. Affective learning is best supported when the learning environment is student centered. The CAST website has extensive examples of UDL-inspired lesson plans for all content areas to reinforce differentiation.

SUMMARY

Special education was born with the belief in the educational rights of all students. The unique needs of diverse students must be clearly defined and education designed to confer benefit. As more students from many backgrounds and abilities are included in general education placements, general education and special education teachers, as well as the other professionals, are working together more closely to support the physical, social, medical, behavioral, language, and academic needs of all students. School teams are coordinating the academic programs of diverse students, using data to make education decisions, setting goals based on the data, and designing instruction that values multiple ways of learning.

REVIEW

1. What are your strengths in working with diverse students? Your concerns?

2. After completing the self-assessment activity using Template 1.1, write one goal to increase your knowledge and skill in working with diverse students.

3. What other roles and responsibilities not listed in Table 1.1 are associated with general education and special education teachers who work with diverse students?

4. After completing Template 1.2, compare and discuss your findings with a colleague.

5. Using the IEP from Template 1.3, identify responsibilities associated with your position.

REFERENCES

Council of Chief State School Officers. (April 2011). Interstate Teacher Assessment and Support Consortium (InTASC) Model Core Teaching Standards: A Resource for State Dialogue. Washington, DC.

Hall, T., Strangman, N., & Meyer, A. (2011). Differentiated Instruction and Implications for UDL Implementation. Retrieved from http://aim.cast.org

IDEA (2004). 20 U.S.C. 1401(3); 1401(30) section 300.8 Child With a Disability.

Office of Special Education and Rehabilitative Services (OSERS), U.S. Department of Education (2004). 34 CFR 300.320 through 300.324.

U.S. Department of Education, National Center for Education Statistics (2012). *Digest of Education Statistics*, 2011.

TEMPLATE 1.1: PATHWAY TO WORKING WITH DIVERSE STUDENTS

Select the column that most closely matches your personal experience and pathway to working with diverse students. Complete the self assessment of skill areas using the following rating system: H = High confidence, M = Medium confidence, L = Low confidence.

SKILL AREAS	4-YEAR DEGREE IN ___, NO OR FEW EDUCATION COURSES.	COMMUNITY EXPERT WHO WORKED FOR YEARS AS A ___; NO OR FEW EDUCATION COURSES.	FULLY LICENSED IN ELEMENTARY OR SECONDARY EDUCATION, NOT SPECIAL EDUCATION.	FULLY LICENSED IN SPECIAL EDUCATION, MAY NOT BE WORKING IN AREA OF DISABILITY EXPERTISE OR GRADE LEVEL.	FULLY LICENSED IN SPECIAL EDUCATION AND A SECONDARY CONTENT AREA OR ELEMENTARY EDUCATION.	SUBSTITUTE OR PARAPROFESSIONAL BEGINNING WORK ON A DEGREE IN SPECIAL EDUCATION OR ENDORSEMENT.
General support & mentoring on all areas of teaching						
Special education laws & disabilities						
District-wide information						
Resources, materials, & technology						
Managing student behaviors						
Classroom organizational skills						
Interactions & communication with others						
Effective instructional practices:						
1. Learner Objectives						
2. Vocabulary						
3. Visual Representations						
4. Student Engagement						
5. Grouping & Cooperative Learning						
6. Asking Questions						
7. Assessment & Grading						

TEMPLATE 1.2: ROLES AND RESPONSIBILITIES OF CLASSROOM PROFESSIONALS

Chapter 1 provides insight into the roles and responsibilities of general education and special education teachers. However, there are many other professionals involved in the success of diverse students. Some, not all, of those who are instrumental partners are listed below.

PROFESSIONAL	ROLES AND RESPONSIBILITIES
ELL Teachers	
Teachers of Gifted and Talented	
Speech Language Pathologists	
School Counselors	
School Psychologists	
Literacy Coaches	
Principals	
Occupational Therapist	
Physical Therapist	
Nurses	
Social Workers	
Behavior Interventionists	

TEMPLATE 1.3: THE IEP

Every state or district has a formalized document used in preparation of the program for a student with a disability. Review the blank IEP template, and locate areas where your roles and responsibilities will be identified.

_____School District

Individual Education Program		**Page 1**

Student Name	Meeting Date	Purpose of Meeting ☐ Initial Eligibility, IEP, Placement ☐ Annual Review of IEP
Student Information Management System (SIMS) Number	Age Grade	☐ Three-Year Reevaluation ☐ Dismissal from Services Date: _____
	Date of Birth	☐ Parent Request ☐ Other:
☐ Male ☐ Female	Date Services Begin	Discussed evaluation results/progress/assessment method ☐ Yes ____ (Parent/Guardian initial)
Ethnicity: (W, B, I, H, A)		Copy of evaluation results received? ☐ Yes ____ (Parent initial)
School of Residence	Annual Review Date	***Transition Planning Needed ☐ No** ☐ **Yes (If yes, attach applicable transition pages)**
Attendance Center	Parent/Guardian Name, Address, Phone	Student is eligible for special education or special education and related services as determined by the IEP team ☐ Yes ☐ No
Date of Eligibility Determination:		An annual copy of Parent/Guardian Rights was received and reviewed _____(Date) _____ (Parent/Guardian Initial)
	Hm: Wk:	
Three-Year Reevaluation Due By:	Parent/Guardian Name, Address, Phone	A copy of the IEP was provided to parent/guardian ☐ Yes _____ (Parent/Guardian Initial)
	Hm: Wk:	

IEP Team Membership	**Signature**	**Date**
Parent/Guardian		
Parent/Guardian		
Student		
Superintendent/Designee		
General Classroom Teacher		
Special Education Teacher		
Speech/Language Pathologist		
Evaluator		
Title		
Title		
Title		

Child Count Information (Required Information)

Disabling Condition

☐ 0500-D/B ☐ 0505-ED ☐ 0510-CD ☐ 0515-HL ☐ 0525-SLD
☐ 0530-MD ☐ 0535-OI ☐ 0540-VL ☐ 0545-D ☐ 0550-S/L
☐ 0555-OHI ☐ 0560-A ☐ 0565-TBI ☐ 0570-DD

A. Minutes per week in Special Education

B. Minutes per week in Related Services

	Minutes	Services
	_____	_____
	_____	_____
	_____	_____
	_____	_____

C. A + B = (Total minutes of Special Education/Related Services) _____

Placement

☐ 0100 General Class with Modifications 80–100%
☐ 0110 Resource Room 40–79%
☐ 0120 Self-Contained Classroom 0–39%
☐ 0130 Separate Day School
☐ 0140 Residential Facility
☐ 0150 Home/Hospital
☐ 0315 Early Childhood Setting 80–100%
☐ 0325 Early Childhood Setting 40–79%
☐ 0330 Early Childhood Setting 0–39%
☐ 0335 Separate Class
☐ 0345 Separate School
☐ 0355 Residential Facility
☐ 0365 Home
☐ 0375 Service Provider Location

Parent/Guardian declines all special education services

Parent/Guardian Signature: _____

Present Levels of Academic Achievement and Functional Performance   Page 2

Based on evaluation, include academic achievement and functional performance (**strengths and weaknesses**) **in the areas affected by the student's disability, including transition** in the IEP to be in effect when the student turns 16; **parent concerns**; and how the student's disability affects the student's **involvement and progress in the general education curriculum.** (For a preschool child, how the disability affects his/her participation in appropriate activities.)

Student Name:	IEP Date:

* Remember to address:
- **Skill or Transition Area (Academic achievement AND functional performance)**
- **Strengths and Needs**
- **How the student's disability affects his/her involvement/progress in the general education curriculum for the skill area**
- **Parent input**

Consideration of Special Factors   Page 3

Is the student limited English proficient? ☐ Yes ☐ No
If the answer to this question is "yes," please explain the language needs of the student, as these needs relate to the student's IEP.
_____
_____
_____

Are there any special communication needs? ☐ Yes ☐ No
If the answer to this question is "yes," what direct instruction will be provided in the student's mode of communication?
_____
_____
_____

Does the student require Braille? ☐ Yes ☐ No
If the answer to this question is "yes," what Braille services will be provided?
_____
_____
_____

Does the student's behavior impede his or her learning or that of others? ☐ Yes ☐ No
If yes, what strategies are required to appropriately address this behavior, including positive behavioral interventions and supports?
_____
_____
_____
_____
_____

Assistive Technology Devices and Services? ☐ Yes ☐ No
If yes, what device or service will be provided? _____
_____

Physical Education: ☐ Regular ☐ Not Required ☐ Adaptive: Refer to Goals/Goals and Objectives

Hearing Aid Maintenance: ☐ Not Applicable ☐ Yes: Personnel Responsible for Monitoring _____
Describe the monitoring process/frequency necessary for maintenance: _____
_____

Assessment

1. ☐ Student will be taking state and district-wide assessments with or without accommodations. (Accommodations will be determined on page 7.) (Annual goals required.)

2. ☐ Student will be taking an alternate assessment. (The alternate assessment is for students working in the alternate achievement standards.) (Annual goal and short-term objectives required.)

   a. Does the student meet the significant cognitive disability criteria? (If no, student is not eligible to take the alternate assessment.) ☐ Yes ☐ No

   b. Explain the reason why the student cannot participate in the regular assessment. _____
   _____
   _____

   c. Explain the reason why the alternate assessment selected is appropriate for this student._____
   _____
   _____

3. ☐ State and/or district-wide assessments are not required at this student's grade level during the course of this annual IEP.

Measurable Postsecondary Goals (MPSGs)—Based on Age-Appropriate Assessment   Page 4A

(Required on or before the student's 16th birthday.) Note: The term "Measurable Postsecondary Goals" replaces "Life Planning Outcomes." (What does the student plan to do after high school?)—Current OSEP guidance requires at least one linked annual goal **AND** at least one service/activity for each MPSG identified. Assessment results should determine which MPSGs are addressed.

Employment: _____

_____(See linked annual goal(s) #_____)

Education: _____

OR_____(See linked annual goal(s) #_____)

Training: _____

_____(See linked annual goal(s) #_____)

Independent Living: (where appropriate) _____

_____(See linked annual goal(s) #_____)

Transition Courses of Study

(Required on or before the student's 16th birthday.) (Complete for the current school year through the planned exit year.)
(Should relate to and help the student to progress toward achievement of the Measurable Postsecondary Goals listed above.)

Grade	Grade	Grade	Grade	Grade

Comments: _____

Transfer of Parent/Guardian Rights. (Must be addressed on or before the 17th birthday.)

Student will turn 17 on _____. Student was informed of this transfer of rights on _____/_____/_____.

Graduation or Completion of an Approved Program (Must be addressed at least one year prior to graduation date.)

Student is to graduate/complete program: (Date) _____/_____/_____
Individualized district specific requirements and remaining courses needed to complete an approved secondary education program:

_____

_____

Summary of Performance—(For students who are graduating with a regular diploma or aging out of special education.)
A summary of the child's academic achievement and functional performance, which shall include recommendations on how to assist the child in meeting the child's postsecondary goals, is required. A suggested form and instructions are available on the SEP website.

One Year Follow-Up—(For students who are graduating, aging out, or dropped out.) Students will be contacted one year after exiting, by a contract agency, to determine their status in regard to employment, postsecondary school, and other outcomes.

Transition Services/Coordinated Set of Activities   Page 4B

These seven categories are from section 300.42 of IDEA 2004.

*Transition Services must be a coordinated set of Activities/Strategies designed within a results-oriented process. This means that the activities are those steps or things that need to happen that will lead to post-school results and help the student achieve their desired postsecondary goals. All of the activities that will need to happen to help students achieve their postsecondary goals cannot be done by the school alone. Thus, the activities should include those things that others (students, families, and the appropriate adult services, agencies, or programs) will need to do. When viewed as a whole, the activities should demonstrate involvement and coordination between schools, students, families and the appropriate adult services, agencies or programs.

Instruction:

Activity Recommendations   Personnel/Agency/Person Responsible   Date Initiated   Date Completed

Related Services:

Activity Recommendations   Personnel/Agency/Person Responsible   Date Initiated   Date Completed

Community Experiences:

Activity Recommendations   Personnel/Agency/Person Responsible   Date Initiated   Date Completed

Employment:

Activity Recommendations   Personnel/Agency/Person Responsible   Date Initiated   Date Completed

Other Post-School Adult Living Objectives:

Activity Recommendations   Personnel/Agency/Person Responsible   Date Initiated   Date Completed

Acquisition of Daily Living Skills (When Appropriate):

Activity Recommendations   Personnel/Agency/Person Responsible   Date Initiated   Date Completed

Functional Vocational Evaluation (When Appropriate):

Activity Recommendations   Personnel/Agency/Person Responsible   Date Initiated   Date Completed

Educational Goals and Objectives/Benchmarks   Page 5

Student Name				Title of Personnel Responsible

Measurable Annual Goal #_____	Proc. Code/s	Date	Prog. Code	Comments:

Short-Term Instructional Objectives or Benchmarks (Required for students who take alternate assessments aligned to alternate achievement standards.)	Proc. Code/s	Date	Prog. Code	Comments:

Accommodations/Modifications/Supplementary Aids and Services	Frequency	Location	Begin Date	Duration
1._____	_____	_____	_____	_____
2._____	_____	_____	_____	_____
3._____	_____	_____	_____	_____
4._____	_____	_____	_____	_____
5._____	_____	_____	_____	_____

Statement of the program modifications or supports for school personnel (as appropriate):	Frequency	Location	Begin Date	Duration

Procedure Codes (Complete at IEP meeting)

1. Teacher-made tests	6. Work samples
2. Observations	7. Portfolios
3. Weekly tests	8. Oral tests
4. Unit tests	9. Data response
5. Student conferences	10. Other:

Progress Codes
P= Progress being made
I= Insufficient progress to meet goal
X= Not addressed this reporting period
M=Met goal

Reporting Frequency to Parents
☐ Quarterly Reports
☐ Trimester Reports ☐ Other: _____
Reporting Method to Parents
☐ Conferences   ☐ Report Card
☐ Goal Page Copy ☐ Other: _____

Related Services to Be Provided   **Page 6**

Related Service to be Provided	Title of Person Responsible	Amount of Service	Location of Service	Duration of Service (If less than duration of IEP)
☐ A. Occupational Therapy				
☐ B. Physical Therapy				
☐ C. Psychological Services				
☐ D. Counseling Services (including rehabilitation counseling)				
☐ E. Social Work Services (in schools)				
☐ F. Audiological Services				
☐ G. Recreation Therapy				
☐ H. School Nurse/Health Services				
☐ I. Speech/Language Therapy				
☐ J. Transportation (Specify when, how often, where, distance, costs, etc.)				
☐ K. Orientation and Mobility				
☐ L. Medical Services (Diagnostic services only)				
☐ M. Interpreting Services				
☐ N. Parent Counseling/Training				
☐ O. Other				

<u>**State/District Assessment Accommodations**</u>   Page 7

1. ☐ Student will be taking the assessment without accommodations.

2. ☐ Student will be taking the assessment with the accommodations.

***Teams must consider if the accommodations are approved for the applicable test administration.**

***List the accommodations the student will be taking for each test/test area.**
(Only those accommodations identified for instruction on the goal pages can be considered for state and district-wide testing. The accommodations selected for use must relate to the student's disability.)

Grades 3–4–5–6–7–8–11 **Dakota STEP** Reading	Grades 5 and 9 **Stanford** Writing	District Specific Tests **Name:** Area(s)
_____	_____	_____
_____	_____	_____
_____	_____	_____
Math	_____	_____
_____	_____	_____
_____	_____	_____
_____	_____	_____
Grades 5–8–11 Science	_____	
_____	_____	_____
_____	_____	_____
_____	_____	_____

* Alternate Assessment
 All accommodations documented in the IEP are allowed to be used for students taking the alternate assessment.

Least Restrictive Environment   Page 8

Continuum of Alternative Placements	**Continuum of Alternative Placements (Ages 3–5)**
☐ 0100 General Classroom with Modifications 80–100%	☐ 0315 Early Childhood Setting 80–100%
☐ 0110 Resource Room 40–79%	☐ 0325 Early Childhood Setting 40–79%
☐ 0120 Self-Contained Classroom 0–39%	☐ 0330 Early Childhood Setting 0–39%
☐ 0130 Separate Day School	☐ 0335 Separate Class
☐ 0140 Residential Facility	☐ 0345 Separate School
☐ 0150 Home/Hospital	☐ 0355 Residential Facility
	☐ 0365 Home
	☐ 0375 Service Provider Location

Special Education to Be Provided:

Description of services	Amount of service	Location of service

Participation with Non-Disabled Peers (Complete for all students ages 6–21)

Program Options		Comments
☐ Art	☐ Vocational Education	
☐ Industrial Technology	☐ Family and Consumer Science	
☐ Music	☐ Other	

Nonacademic		Comments
☐ Counseling	☐ Recess	
☐ Meals	☐ Health Services	
☐ Employment Referrals	☐ Other_____	

Extracurricular		Comments
☐ Athletics	☐ Recreation	
☐ Clubs	☐ Other_____	
☐ Groups		

Justification for Placement—An explanation of the extent, if any, to which the child will not participate with non-disabled children in regular classes and nonacademic activities. (Please use accept/reject format for each alternative placement considered.)

☐ *The team addressed the potential harmful effects of the special education placement.*

Extended School Year   Page 9

Extended School Year Services: ☐ Needed ☐ Not needed ☐ To be determined by (date) ____ / ____ / ____

Goal(s) #	*Type of Service	Beginning Date mm/dd/yy	Ending Date mm/dd/yy	Minutes per Week	**Based on

*   Instruction, related services (specify), other (list)

** Regression/Recoupment, Emerging Skills, or Maintenance of Critical Life Skills

Parent/Guardian Consent Required For Initial Placement Only

"Consent" means that the parent(s)/guardian(s) have been fully informed of all information relevant to the activity for which consent is sought, in the native language, or other mode of communication; the parent(s)/guardian(s) understand and agree in writing to the carrying out of the activity for which consent is sought, and the consent describes that activity and lists any records which will be released and to whom; and the granting of consent by the parent(s)/guardian(s) is voluntary and may be revoked in writing at any time.

_____
Parent/Guardian Signature   Date

Clarifying Comments:

TEMPLATE 1.4: IEP AT A GLANCE

Use this form to highlight and summarize the IEP requirements for a student with a disability who will be in an inclusive general education classroom.

Student:	Identification Number:
Grade:	Date:
Teacher(s):	Class:

Goals Linked to Common Core Standards: *(Specific to the class)*

Instructional Accommodations:

Assessment Accommodations:

Accommodations to the Environment:

TEMPLATE 1.5: AN ACRONYM JOURNAL

Begin keeping a personal journal of acronyms to assist in communicating with others about diverse students with whom you work. You may want to expand this to include terms you are unfamiliar with and legal language. For example, Due Process would align with letter "D" and the definition would follow on the corresponding line.

ACRONYMS, TERMS, OR LEGAL LANGUAGE	DEFINITIONS
A	
B	
C	
D	
E	
F	
G	
H	
I	
J	
K	
L	
M	
N	
O	
P	
Q	
R	
S	
T	
U	
V	
W	
X	
Y	
Z	

Chapter two

LEARNER OBJECTIVES

*My greatest satisfaction comes when my students find the success they
never thought they could have.*

—ADDIE RHODES LEE

OBJECTIVES

Readers will be able to:

1. Create and implement content objectives.

2. Create and implement language objectives.

3. Write and modify learning objectives to meet the needs and abilities of all students
   in a general education classroom.

KEY VOCABULARY

Readers will be able to define or describe each term in the context of the chapter information.

Content Objective	Language Rigor	Language Objective
Learning Verbs	Product Options	Student Independence
Modified Objective	Learner Objective	Teacher Objective

INTRODUCTION

"Would you tell me, please, which way I ought to go from here?" said Alice. "That depends a good deal on where you want to get to," said the Cat. "I don't much care where," said Alice. "Then it doesn't matter which way you go," said the Cat *(Alice's Adventures in Wonderland)*.

Can you imagine a classroom teacher coming into the classroom without a student learning objective and route? Without student learning objectives, classroom teachers are much like Alice. In other words, if there are no learning objectives, then it doesn't really matter which lesson is presented to the students. It can be argued that having well-defined objectives, focusing on identified standards, may be the most important part of a lesson plan.

Successful classroom teachers understand the importance of having a solid lesson plan. They know that an effective lesson plan, in addition to fostering student success, can greatly reduce, or even eliminate, negative class management issues. An effective lesson plan can foster significant student learning (Orlich, Harder, Callahan, & Gibson, 2009; Anspaugh & Ezell, 2007; Wentz, 2006). An effective lesson plan can also increase student motivation, engagement, and an overall positive learning environment.

Creating an effective lesson plan can be a challenging task—especially for the beginning teacher (Orlich, Harder, Callahan, & Gibson, 2009; Goethals, Howard, & Sanders, 2003). However, most teachers soon realize the benefits of having a comprehensive lesson plan. An effective lesson plan takes into account the diversity of learners in the class.

Learner objectives—based on appropriate national, state, and/or district standards—are a critical part of every lesson plan. There are several other important components in lesson plans. These include key vocabulary, targeted language modalities (reading, writing, listening, speaking), grouping formats, scaffolding techniques, transitions, and assessment practices.

What Are Learner Objectives?

Learner objectives specifically describe what students are expected to know or be able to do as the result of instruction. Learner objectives are typically focused on one specific lesson. There is an important difference between learner objectives and instructional objectives. Instructional objectives describe what the teacher will do, such as give a mini-lecture, show a video, divide the class into small study groups, or facilitate journal entries. Instructional objectives answer the two questions, "What will the teacher and students be doing?" and "How long will they be doing it?" On the other hand, learner objectives answer the question, "What will the students know or be able to do?"

What Is the Purpose of Learner Objectives?

Learner objectives set the instructional target for teachers and the learning target for students. As educators, we cannot hit a student learning target we never set. Students cannot hit a learning target they never set. Learner objectives define the degree of rigor expected and needed to successfully achieve the targeted objective. This defined rigor will assist the teacher in deciding which teaching strategy and learning activity will most likely produce the desired student results.

What Are the Attributes of a Learner Objective?

Writing effective learner objectives usually takes a little practice. There are seven important guidelines to consider when writing learner objectives.

1. Language: Learner objectives should be written in student-friendly language.

2. Clear: The objectives should be easily understood and not confusing.

3. Concise: The objectives should be stated in a few meaningful words.

4. Specific: The objectives should be precise and accurate.

5. Relevant: The objectives should be authentic and directly connected with the content and the student.

6. Attainable: The objectives should be realistically possible and achievable.

7. Measurable: The objectives should be assessable and quantifiable.

What Are the Main Types of Learner Objectives?

There are two primary types of learner objectives: content objectives and language objectives. Content and language objectives are important elements for most lessons. However, they are critical elements for lessons in classroom where struggling learners exist. Most commonly, these struggling learners are special education students, English-language learners, or other students with various learning barriers.

Content objectives define the essential targeted knowledge and skill of the discipline (Rohwer & Wandberg, 2005). This targeted knowledge and skill is typically character-ized by facts, concepts, and/or skills. Content objectives are generated and derived from several sources. In most content areas, these sources include National Content Standards, State Education Content Standards or Guidelines (Common Core State Standards, in many states), local school district education content standards or guidelines, and in some instances, teacher-developed content standards or guidelines. Language objectives define the language domains needed to make the content of the discipline comprehensible to students (Rohwer & Wandberg, 2005). These language domains include reading, writing, listening, and speaking. Therefore, language objectives should contain the terms reading, writing, listening, or speaking—or synonyms for these terms, such as tell instead of speak. If a teacher were to use the term "explain" in a language objective, it could be written as "explain in writing" or "explain by telling."

Language objectives often focus on a variety of language skills. These include skills such as:

1. Developing students' content-related vocabulary;

2. Developing and practicing reading comprehension skills;

3. Revising and editing;

4. Verb tenses, capitalization, outlining, grammar;

5. Brainstorming;

6. Requesting information;

7. Giving directions;

8. Providing explanations;

9. Summarizing information;

10. Comparing or contrasting information;

11. Basic language mechanics.

While teachers frequently address content objectives in their lessons, they rarely discuss language objectives. Language objectives are crucial in classrooms where students are struggling with language issues. English-language learners, some special education learners, and other struggling learners can more easily master content when teaching practices incorporate strategies for language learning, like the use of language objectives (Dong, 2005).

How Often Should Teachers Prepare and Write Learner Objectives?

This is one of the most frequently asked questions, and it has the shortest answer. Teachers should prepare learner objectives for every academic lesson. Academic lessons vary in length. Elementary-level lessons may be relatively short, whereas middle school and high school lessons, especially in schools that are on an extended block schedule format, may run for around 90 minutes. In some instances, the learner objectives could cover more than one class meeting. Remember, we are speaking about lessons, not units. Academic units are typically made up of several academic lessons.

How Might a Teacher Visualize a Learner Objective?

Here is one way many teachers think about learner objectives. Based on the student standards and benchmarks they are targeting and the curricular scope and sequence they are following, the teachers determine specifically what the students should know and/or be able to do as a result of the anticipated lesson. In other words, what is it that the students probably don't know (or are able to do) when they enter the lesson or classroom and you expect them to know (or be able to do) when they leave the lesson or exit the classroom?

How Should Content and Language Objectives Be Presented to Students?

Both content objectives and language objectives should be provided to students every instructional day, using two critical instructional techniques:

1. Students should be able to see (in written form) and hear (orally) their content and language objectives prior to instruction. For the oral component, either the teacher or a student can read the objectives for the entire class to hear. It is also recommended that those objectives stay visible throughout the entire lesson. Teachers are then able to refer back to them periodically during the lesson. Some teachers who use PowerPoint presentations split the presentation screen so that the learning objective is on one side of the screen, and the academic content is on the other. Some teachers split their PowerPoint screens top and bottom rather than right and left.

2. Students should have the opportunity to ask clarifying questions about their learning objectives prior to instruction. For example, if a teacher presented a language objective focused on writing, students will often ask, "Does spelling count?"

What Are the Steps in Writing Effective Learner Objectives?

Step 1: Determine the Learner Objective Sentence Starter

Many state and local education departments use universal learner objective sentence starters. A common learner objective sentence starter is "Students will be able to" (SWBAT). However, in an effort to personalize the content and language objectives in the classroom to students, many teachers choose to use "You will be able to" (YWBAT) as their objective starter. In some instances, a learning condition precedes the objective sentence starter. Examples of learning conditions are

1.   After completing the worksheet, SWBAT ...

2.   After viewing the video, SWBAT ...

3.   Following the media presentation, SWBAT ...

4.   After hearing the speaker, SWBAT ...

5.   After reading the article, SWBAT ...

6.   Following the class discussion, SWBAT ...

Step 2: Add the Learning Verb

Teachers often indicate that selecting the most appropriate learning verb is one of the most difficult parts of writing an effective learner objective. There are dozens of learning verbs. Learning verbs range from low cognitive demand (e.g., list, tell, name) to higher cognitive demand (e.g., judge, defend, recommend, critique). Commonly, the verbs are identified in a range of five levels. Level 1 represents the lowest cognitive demand, Level 5 the highest cognitive demand. See Table 2.1.

Step 3: Determine the Learner Objective

The learner objective clearly describes what the student needs to do to demonstrate his or her learning.

Sample Content Objectives:

Example 1: SWBAT create a visual representation of the solar system.

Example 2: SWBAT use a spreadsheet to calculate survey data.

Example 3: SWBAT create a Venn diagram that compares and contrasts the basic structures and functions of two government agencies listed in the assigned reading.

Table 2.1 Sample List of Learning Verbs

COGNITIVE LEVEL	SAMPLE VERBS
Cognitive Verbs, Level 1	List, name, circle, point, draw, label, underline, locate, match, choose, state, tell
Cognitive Verbs, Level 2	Explain, describe, prepare, draw, restate, summarize, infer, express, report, discuss
Cognitive Verbs, Level 3	Apply, solve, show, classify, illustrate, operate, plan, modify, demonstrate, transfer
Cognitive Verbs, Level 4	Create, invent, compose, design, predict, organize, improve, formulate, produce, imagine
Cognitive Verbs, Level 5	Judge, select, decide, justify, verify, rank, validate, defend, score, evaluate, critique, assess

How Should Content Objectives Be Written?

Remember, content objectives are obtained from sources that include National Content Standards, State Education Content Standards or Guidelines (Common Core State Standards, in many states), and local school district education content standards or guidelines.

Example 1: SWBAT solve word problems involving addition of two single-digit numbers.

Example 2: SWBAT identify and cite specific evidence in the assigned reading to support analysis of primary and secondary sources.

How Should Language Objectives Be Written?

As stated earlier, language objectives describe how the student will demonstrate the achievement of the content objective using the four language modalities of reading, writing, listening, and speaking. In the language objective examples below, you will notice the italicized terms that focus specifically on the language modalities. At least one (sometimes more) of these four language modalities (or a synonymous term) should be in every language learner objective. For instance, a teacher may wish to substitute the term "tell" for "speaking."

From time to time, many teachers find language statements and prompts helpful in writing language objectives. See Table 2.2.

Table 2.2 Sample Language Statements and Prompts Content Examples

LANGUAGE STATEMENTS AND PROMPTS	CONTENT EXAMPLE
Language Focus	**Students will be able to:**
Read and answer	Read the article on election fraud and answer the two questions.
Read and discuss	Read the three astronomy statements and discuss their accuracy.
Read and summarize	Read the pamphlet on AIDS and summarize, in writing, the two main ideas.
Read and outline	Read the booklet on how presidents are elected and outline the information.
Read out loud	Taking paragraph turns, read out loud the article on exercise.
Write a paragraph	Write a paragraph on one of the benefits of exercise.
Write a sentence	Write a sentence using the word "population."
Write a paper	Write a 200–300 word paper summarizing how a bill becomes law.
Use correct grammar	Use correct grammar when writing the story about safety in your home.
Take notes	Take notes on the main ideas presented while listening to the guest speaker.
Listen to the video	Listen to the video and complete the biographical outline.
Write the steps	In correct order, write the steps for performing CPR.
Tell a partner	Tell a partner how to write equations in quadratic form.
State the meaning	Explain the meaning of the word "probability."
With your partner, explain	With your partner, explain to the class the three different advertising techniques.
Give an example	Give an example of a carcinogen in tobacco and/or tobacco smoke.
Give the definition	To your partner, give the definition of a prime number.
Ask a question	After viewing the film on the solar system, ask a question.
Give an opinion	Give you opinion: Are there limits to confidentiality?

Sample Content Language Objectives:

Example 1: SWBAT *orally* summarize, in their own words, the plot of the story.

Example 2: SWBAT *write* and record observations.

Example 3: SWBAT *read and orally* explain the Nutrition Facts Panel.

Some teachers find it advantageous to add a statement describing the standard or degree needed for successful completion of the learner objective. Examples include "at least 90 percent accuracy"; "according to accepted scientific method"; "a minimum rubric score of 15"; "at least five"; or "in the correct sequence."

Example 1

Basic Objective:

SWBAT produce an essay that describes parallels between Story 1 and Story 2.

Objective with Degree:

SWBAT produce a five-paragraph essay that describes four parallels between Story 1 and Story 2.

Example 2

Basic Objective:

SWBAT define the four highlighted terms in the article.

Objective with Degree:

SWBAT accurately define the four highlighted terms in the article.

Objective with Degree:

SWBAT define the four highlighted terms in the article with 100 percent accuracy.

In summary, to write an effective learner objective—either content or language—simply fill in the five columns in Table 2.3. Also, for additional support, see the template at the end of this chapter (Template 2.1: Writing Content and Language Objectives).

Table 2.3 Writing Learner Objectives

CONDITION	STARTER (SWBAT)	VERB	MEASURABILITY	CONTENT
After viewing the video	students will be able to	list	in order, the first four	presidents of the United States.

How Can Teachers Modify Learner Objectives?

A single general education classroom often contains a wide variety of student learners. In the classroom, there may be special education learners, English-language learners, special education students, gifted learners, and the wide range of "on-level" learners. In terms of language proficiency and other learning abilities, learner objectives often need to be modified (differentiated) to more closely match the needs and proficiencies of the student(s). Modifying objectives is one of several methods of "differentiating" the instructional teaching strategies and learning activities. Both content and language objectives can be modified using the same strategy.

Modifying students' learning objectives is one of several critical instructional strategies needed to promote and maximize high-level student learning and achievement in learning-diverse classrooms. It is important to remember that the purpose of modification is to match the objective's rigor to the needs and abilities of the student(s). For this reason, the process of "modification" may require the modified objective to be either of higher learning rigor (in the case of higher-ability students) or of lower learning rigor (in the case of struggling students). In other words, not all modifications should result in a lower student rigor. Higher rigor may be the more appropriate! In addition, it's important to remember that as students become more confident and demonstrate successful achievement, the level of rigor can—and should—be changed.

There are three basic steps to help teachers modify learner objectives.

Step 1—Determine the students' language and/or ability proficiencies.

Step 2—Determine whether or not the learner objectives need modification.

Step 3—Determine which instructional technique will be used to modify the learner objectives.

Step 1—Determine the Students' Language and Ability Proficiencies

Many schools and school districts have special education, English-language learner, and gifted student specialists and others who can assist teachers in determining the language and ability proficiencies of their students. They can also assist in suggesting educational approaches designed to meet the students' needs and abilities.

Step 2—Determine Whether or Not the Learner Objectives Need Modification

Using the educational professionals described in Step 1, teachers should be able to obtain the necessary information concerning the language and/or ability proficiencies of their students. With this information, the teacher can then decide whether or not the lesson's learner objectives need modification.

Step 3—Determine Which Instructional Technique Will Be Used to Modify the Learner Objective

There are three basic instructional techniques used to modify learner objectives:

Technique 1: Reduce or increase the language rigor.

Technique 2: Reduce or increase student independence.

Technique 3: Provide product options.

Depending on the specific needs and abilities of the students, applying two or more modification techniques to a single learner objective may be necessary to achieve the desired result.

Instructional Technique 1: Reduce or Increase the Language Rigor

Reduce or increase the language rigor by changing the verb describing the learner outcome.

Example:

"Students will be able to *demonstrate* three exercises that build muscle and help promote loss of body fat."

In this example, the language rigor verb is "demonstrate." Using Table 2.4 as a guide, the teacher can easily select the most appropriate modification terms.

Table 2.4 Sample Modification Verbs

COGNITIVE LEVEL	REDUCE THE RIGOR	INCREASE THE RIGOR	SAMPLE VERBS
Cognitive Verbs, Level 1			List, name, circle, point, draw, label, underline, locate, match, choose, state, tell
Cognitive Verbs, Level 2			Explain, describe, prepare, draw, restate, summarize, infer, express, report, discuss
Cognitive Verbs, Level 3			Apply, solve, show, classify, illustrate, operate, plan, modify, demonstrate, transfer
Cognitive Verbs, Level 4			Create, invent, compose, design, predict, organize, improve, formulate, produce, imagine
Cognitive Verbs, Level 5			Judge, select, decide, justify, verify, rank, validate, defend, score, evaluate, critique, assess

Examples to <u>reduce</u> the language rigor:

Example 1: "Students will be able to *name* three exercises that build muscle and help promote loss of body fat."

Example 2: "Students will be able to *identify* three exercises that build muscle and help promote loss of body fat."

Examples to <u>increase</u> the language rigor:

Example 1: "Students will be able to *create* three exercises that build muscle and help promote loss of body fat."

Example 2: "Students will be able to *prioritize* three exercises that build muscle and help promote loss of body fat."

Teachers should always match student assessment items with the objective's language rigor. (See Chapter 7 for additional information.) For example, it would be inappropriate for a student to have a specific learner objective's language rigor as "list" and the corresponding assessment's language rigor as "prioritize."

Instructional Technique 2: Reduce or Increase Student Independence

There are also several ways to increase or decrease the independence rigor. In this case, the teacher will focus on the level of student dependence. A common four-category range of student dependence is:

- Independent—the student works alone

- Partner—the student works with one other student

- Small Group—the student works with four to six other students

- Whole Class—the student works with the entire class.

Example:

With a *partner*, students will be able to place the story's major events in chronological order.

In this example the level of student independence term is "partner." Using Table 2.5 as a guide, the teacher can easily select the most appropriate modification terms.

Table 2.5 Changing the Independence Level

INSTRUCTION TYPE	REDUCE THE INDEPENDENCE LEVEL	INCREASE THE INDEPENDENCE LEVEL
Whole Class		
Small Group		
Partner		
Independent Work		

Example to <u>reduce</u> the independence rigor:

In a *small group*, students will be able to place the story's major events in chrono-logical order.

Example to <u>increase</u> the independence rigor:

Students will be able to *independently* place the story's major events in chrono-logical order.

Instructional Technique 3: Provide Product Options

Scenario 1: Consider a teacher who wants his students to learn and know about the history of AIDS. The teacher assigns students a written report with six specific components/criteria:

1.   Written component;

2.   Appropriate vocabulary;

3.   Organized and focused;

4.   Proper grammar;

5.   Neat and presentable;

6.   Proper references.

   One of the students, Alejandra, struggles with the English language. This is especially true with her writing skills. She really enjoys this class. She is interested in learning about the history of AIDS. When she learns of the teacher's <u>WRITING</u> assignment, she feels defeated before she even starts the assignment. By reading and speaking with others, she is able to learn much about the history of AIDS, but her confidence in her writing skills is making this assignment appear hopeless. Predicting defeat, Alejandra chooses to skip the assignment.

Scenario 2: Consider a teacher who wants her students to learn what influences a person's food choices. The teacher assigns all students an oral presentation with five specific oral component criteria:

1.   Appropriate speaking volume;

2.   Appropriate speaking speed;

3.   Appropriate eye contact;

4.   Actively involves the audience;

5.   Creative and interesting.

One of the students, Reid, is fearful of speaking in front of others. He gets nervous and his whole body shakes. When he learns of the teacher's assignment, he feels ill. He likes the subject of nutrition and is excited about learning more about what influences food choices. He knows that there are probably many influences, including physical, psychological, cultural, friends, and the media. But because the teacher would only accept the information in a speech format, Reid, like Alejandra, chooses to skip the assignment. He would rather take the "failure" than to face the embarrassment in front of his friends.

In both Scenarios 1 and 2, the students were eager to learn more about the topic. However, in these two scenarios, the teachers would only accept the "proof" or "documentation" of learning in one way—writing in Scenario 1 and speaking in Scenario 2. Neither scenario had a positive educational outcome for the student.

How could these two scenarios be modified to increase the likelihood of a positive educational outcome for Alejandra and Reid? In other words, what other ways could Alejandra and Reid demonstrate their learning of the topic?

Review the list of sample product options in Table 2.6. Which of these options may have been viable for Alejandra and Reid?

For many learner objectives, there may be multiple ways (products) students could demonstrate and prove their learning of the objective. Granted, some learner objectives may be so specific that multiple demonstrations may not be possible. However, whenever it is possible, teachers should try to offer product options. Providing product options is another excellent way to modify learner objectives to better meet the needs and abilities of students.

Table 2.6 Sample Product Options

Write a report	Build a Model	Create a cartoon
Draw	Construct a diagram	Survey
Orally explain	Create a poster	Create a song
Teach a lesson	Conduct an experiment	Write a poem
Make a game	Create a video	Create a commercial
••••Plus many more••••		

SUMMARY

Most classrooms contain students with a wide variety of learning proficiencies. These proficiencies may vary, based on language, disability, and other factors. One of the most important first steps in planning for these diverse learning classrooms is the creation of targeted student learning objectives. There are two kinds of learning objectives that should be considered: (1) content objectives; and (2) language objectives. Content objectives define the essential intended knowledge of the discipline. These objectives are commonly found in the specific discipline's national and/or state standards. Language objectives define the language skills (e.g., reading, writing, listening, speaking) needed to make the content of the discipline comprehensible.

There are three common ways to modify a content objective and/or a language objective to better meet the needs and abilities of the student(s). One way is to increase or decrease the language rigor. This is done by replacing the objective's cognitive verb to a higher or lower cognitive level. Another way is to increase or decrease the students' independence level. These levels commonly include whole group, small group, partner, and individual. The third way to modify a content and/or language objective is to provide product options. In other words, offer a variety of ways that a student can demonstrate his or her understanding of the desired objective.

REVIEW

1. Describe several differences and similarities in content and language objectives.

2. Accurately describe the steps in creating an effective learner objective.

3. Give two examples of a content objective.

4. Give two examples of a language objective that supports (aligns with) the two content objectives identified in review activity #3.

5. Give an example of three different instructional techniques to modify objectives.

6. Complete the five templates at the end of this chapter.

REFERENCES

Anspaugh, D. J., & Ezell, G. (2007). *Teaching today's health* (8th ed.). San Francisco: Pearson/Benjamin Cummings.

Dong, Y. R. (2005). Getting at the content. *Educational Leadership*, 62(4):14–19.

Goethals, M. S., Howard, R. A., and Sanders, M. M. (2003). *Student teaching: A process to reflective practice* (2nd ed.). Upper Saddle River, NJ: Prentice-Hall Inc.

Orlich, D. C., Harder, R. J., Callahan, R. C., and Gibson, H. (2009). *Teaching strategies: A guide to better instruction* (2nd ed.). Lexington, MA: Houghton Mifflin.

Rohwer, J., and Wandberg, R. (2005). Improving health education for ELL students in the mainstream classroom. *American Journal of Health Education*, 36(3): 155–160.

Wentz, P. J. (2006). *The student teaching experience: Cases for the classroom*. Upper Saddle River, NJ: Merrill/Prentice Hall.

TEMPLATE 2.1: WRITING CONTENT AND LANGUAGE OBJECTIVES

Step 1: Select a grade, course, and unit of your choice.

Step 2: Using each of the five components in the grid below, write five objectives that support your selected grade, course, and unit. Use a variety of low and high level verbs.

Grade (e.g. 8): _____

Course: (e.g. Algebra): _____

Unit: (e.g. Exponents): _____

CONDITION	STARTER	VERB	MEASURABILITY	CONTENT
1.				
2.				
3.				
4.				
5.				

TEMPLATE 2.2: CONTENT AND LANGUAGE OBJECTIVE ALIGNMENT

Step 1: Select a grade, course, and unit of your choice.
Step 2: List six content objectives used in your selected grade, course, and unit.
Step 3: Write six corresponding language objectives that support the corresponding content objectives.

Grade (e.g. 3): _____
Course: (e.g. Language Arts): _____
Unit: (e.g. Phonics): _____

CONTENT OBJECTIVE	LANGUAGE OBJECTIVE
1.	1.
2.	2.
3.	3.
4.	4.
5.	5.
6.	6.

TEMPLATE 2.3: COGNITIVE RANGE OBJECTIVES

Step 1: Select a grade, course, and unit of your choice.
Step 2: Using the information and tables in Chapter 2, write a content and corresponding language objective associated with your selected grade, course, and unit that supports the verbs associated with each cognitive level.

Grade (e.g. 5): _____
Course: (e.g. Math): _____
Unit: (e.g. Fractions): _____

COGNITIVE LEVEL	CONTENT OBJECTIVE	LANGUAGE OBJECTIVE
Level 1		
Level 2		
Level 3		
Level 4		
Level 5		
Level 6		

TEMPLATE 2.4: LANGUAGE FUNCTION OBJECTIVES

Step 1: Select a grade, course, and unit of your choice.
Step 2: Using the information and tables in Chapter 2, write a content or language objective that supports your selected grade, course, and unit and the corresponding language function verb.

Grade (e.g. 8): _____
Course: (e.g. Math): _____
Unit: (e.g. Probability): _____

LANGUAGE FUNCTION	CONTENT OR LANGUAGE OBJECTIVE
Explain	
Locate	
Compare	
Apply	
Categorize	
Predict	
Modify	
Justify	
Synthesize	
Analyze	
Evaluate	

TEMPLATE 2.5: MODIFYING OBJECTIVES

Step 1: Select a grade, course, and unit of your choice.
Step 2: In column 1, write six mid-level content or language objectives that support your selected grade, course, and unit.
Step 3: In column 2, write a corresponding objective that reduces the rigor in language, independence, or product.
Step 4: In column 3, write a corresponding objective that increases the rigor in language, independence, or product.

Grade (e.g. 7): _____
Course: (e.g. Language Arts): _____
Unit: (e.g. Writing Narratives): _____

BASIC OBJECTIVE	REDUCED RIGOR OBJECTIVE	INCREASED RIGOR OBJECTIVE
1.		
2.		
3.		
4.		
5.		
6.		

Chapter three
VOCABULARY

Direct instruction in vocabulary influences comprehension more than any other factor.

—PETER FISHER, 2004

OBJECTIVES

Readers will be able to:

1. Plan, implement, and evaluate a variety of appropriate vocabulary strategies.

2. Reduce the barriers to learning created by multiple-meaning words.

3. Scrutinize lessons containing multiple-meaning words.

4. Plan, implement, and evaluate vocabulary strategies and activities specifically for multiple-meaning words, prefixes, suffixes, and roots.

KEY VOCABULARY

Readers will be able to define or describe each term in the context of the chapter information.

Alphalary	Oral Vocabulary	Print Vocabulary
Frayer Model	Pictograph	Root
Homograph	Prediction Chart	Suffix
Homophone	Prefix	Vocabulary
Multiple-Meaning Words		

INTRODUCTION

It's Monday morning, and Blake has arrived at her middle school ready and excited to be in each of her six classes today. Blake has experienced some learning difficulties in the past, and most of his teachers see her as a "struggling" learner.

Blake's schedule for the day is:

Period 1 Music

Period 2 Geography

Period 3 Physical Education

Period 4 Science

Period 5 Math

Period 6 Language Arts

During Period 1, Blake's music teacher tells the students that the vocabulary word for the day is "pitch," and they need to remember it. She writes this definition on the board: "The degree of highness or lowness of a sound or tone." The teacher then indicates that notes in music with a low pitch have a slower rate of vibration than those with a high pitch. And finally, the teacher informs the students that the particular standard of pitch for voices and instruments is now generally accepted as 440 vibrations per second for A (the first *A* above *Middle C*).

In Blake's next class, geography, the teacher is describing the difficulty of driving on roads in mountains with a very steep pitch. He asks the students, "What does 'pitch' mean? Blake gets to go outside and play softball for her Period 3 physical education class. The teacher is explaining some of the vocabulary words associated with this sport. He asks his class what word describes the act of throwing the ball to the batter. Most of the students responded, "pitch."

After lunch, Blake is off to her Period 4 class, science. The topic is how airplanes can fly. At one point, the teacher discusses how wind and other factors might cause the plane to "pitch." He is referring to the movement of the longitudinal axis of the airplane up or down from the horizontal plane.

Math class is next. After a group activity, the teacher asks all of the students to "pitch" in and help clean up the instructional materials.

The last class of the day is language arts. The teacher is reading a story to the students about a young boy making a sales "pitch" to his parents in an effort to persuade them to buy him a new CD.

That evening, Blake asks her parents what the word "pitch" means.

What Is Vocabulary?

Though we often speak of vocabulary as if it were a single thing, it is not; human beings acquire four types of vocabulary. They are: listening, speaking, reading, and writing. Listening vocabulary, the largest, is made up of words we can hear and understand. All other vocabularies are subsets of our listening vocabulary. The second-largest vocabulary, speaking vocabulary, is comprised of words we can use when we speak. Next is our reading vocabulary, or words we can identify and understand when we read. The smallest is our writing vocabulary, or words we use in writing. These four vocabularies are continually nurtured in the effective teacher's classroom (D. R. Reutzel, 2004).

The term "vocabulary" actually has many definitions. This wide variety of definitions is often dependent on the context in which the term is used. In a general sense, vocabulary is the collection of all the words in a language and their associated meanings. In a personal sense, vocabulary is one's knowledge of words and word meanings. Included in most definitions of "vocabulary" is the word, "word." The *New Oxford American Dictionary* defines "word" as a single distinct meaningful element of speech or writing, used with others (or sometimes alone) to form a sentence and typically shown with a space on either side when written or printed. One must remember that there are oral and print vocabularies. As mentioned earlier, oral vocabulary includes those words that we recognize and use in listening and speaking. Print vocabulary includes those words that we recognize and use in reading and writing. As you may remember in Chapter 2, these terms—reading, writing, listening, and speaking—are the key language modalities and serve as the foundation in a lesson's language objectives.

According to Graves (2009), we all have several different vocabularies. Vocabulary can be classified as receptive (words we understand when others use them) and productive (words we use ourselves). The different vocabularies are:

- Words we understand when we hear them

- Words we can read

- Words we use in our speech

- Words we use in our writing

So, what is vocabulary? In the context of student learning, a student's vocabulary consists of all of the words he or she uses and understands in reading, writing, listening, and speaking. In terms of instruction, educators should strive to increase student vocabulary in all four language domains.

Why Is Vocabulary an Important Component of Content Comprehension?

The connection between reading comprehension and word knowledge has been clear for many years. According to Davis (1968), "vocabulary knowledge is related to and affects comprehension. The relationship between word knowledge and comprehension is unequivocal."

The importance of vocabulary is also attested to by a huge body of empirical evidence (Graves, 1986, 2006, 2007) Among the data-based claims that can be made about word knowledge are these:

- Vocabulary knowledge in kindergarten and first grade is a significant predictor of reading comprehension in the middle and secondary grades.

- Vocabulary difficulty strongly influences the readability of text.

- The vocabulary we use strongly influences judgments of our competence.

- Teaching vocabulary can improve reading comprehension.

- Growing up in poverty can seriously restrict the vocabulary children learn before beginning school and make attaining an adequate vocabulary a very challenging task.

- Learning English vocabulary is one of the most crucial tasks for English learners.

- Lack of vocabulary can be a crucial factor underlying the school failure of many students.

Of the many compelling reasons for providing students with instruction to build vocabulary, none is more important than the contribution of vocabulary knowledge to reading comprehension. Indeed, one of the most enduring findings in reading research is the extent to which students' vocabulary knowledge relates to their reading comprehension (Anderson & Freebody, 1981; Baumann, Kame'enui, & Ash, 2003; Becker, 1977; Davis, Whipple, 1925).

Most recently, the National Reading Panel (2000) concluded that comprehension development cannot be understood without a critical examination of the role played by vocabulary knowledge. Given that students' success in school and beyond depends in great measure upon their ability to read with comprehension, there is an urgency to providing instruction that equips students with the skills and strategies necessary for lifelong vocabulary development. In addition, the National Reading Panel (2000) has put forth eight statements:

1. There is a need for direct instruction of vocabulary items required for a specific text.

2. Repetition and multiple exposure to vocabulary items are important. Students should be given items that will likely appear in many contexts.

3. Learning in rich contexts is valuable for vocabulary learning. Vocabulary words should be those that the learner will find useful in many contexts. When vocabulary items are derived from content learning materials, the learner will be better equipped to deal with specific reading matter in content areas.

4. Vocabulary tasks should be restructured as necessary. It is important to be certain that students fully understand what is asked of them in the context of reading, rather than focusing only on the words to be learned. Restructuring seems to be most effective for low-achieving or at-risk students.

5. Vocabulary learning is effective when it entails active engagement in learning tasks.

6. Computer technology can be used effectively to help teach vocabulary.

7. Vocabulary can be acquired through incidental learning. Much of a student's vocabulary will have to be learned in the course of doing things other than explicit vocabulary learning. Repetition, richness of context, and motivation may also add to the efficacy of incidental learning of vocabulary.

8. Dependence on a single vocabulary instruction method will not result in optimal learning. A variety of methods was used effectively, with emphasis on multimedia aspects of learning, richness of context in which words are to be learned, and the number of exposures to words that learners receive.

One of the most persistent findings in reading research is that the extent of students' vocabulary knowledge relates strongly to their reading comprehension and overall academic success (Baumann, Kame'enui, & Ash, 2003; Becker, 1977; Davis, 1944; Whipple, 1925). This relationship seems logical; to get meaning from what they read, students need both a great many words in their vocabularies and the ability to use various strategies to establish the meanings of new words when they encounter them. Young students who don't have large vocabularies or effective word-learning strategies often struggle to achieve comprehension. Their bad experiences with reading set in motion a cycle of frustration and failure that continues throughout their schooling (Hart & Risley, 2003; Snow, Barnes, Chandler, Goodman, & Hemphill, 2000; White, Graves, & Slater, 1990). Because these students don't have sufficient word knowledge to understand what they read, they typically avoid reading. Because they don't read very much, they don't have the opportunity to see and learn very many new words. This sets in motion the well-known "Matthew effects," Stanovich's (1986) application of Matthew 25:29—"the rich get richer and the poor get poorer." In terms of vocabulary development, good readers read more, become better readers, and learn more words; poor readers read less, become poorer readers, and learn fewer words.

The extensive research base on vocabulary learning and teaching provides us with important guidelines that inform instruction (Harmon, Wood, & Hedrick, in press). In their research summary, they highlight relevant studies that support several key understandings of vocabulary learning and teaching. The following are six key understandings for all teachers across age levels and content areas.

1. Word knowledge is important for learning.

2. Word knowledge is complex.

3. Metacognition is an important aspect of vocabulary learning.

4. Effective vocabulary instruction moves beyond the definitional level of word meanings.

5. Vocabulary learning occurs implicitly in classrooms across disciplines.

6. Vocabulary learning occurs through direct instruction.

How Many Words Are Students Exposed to, and How Many Do They Need to Know?

Did you know that "hyperpolysyllabicomania" means a fondness for big words? Often, it's not the "big" words that challenge students, it's the everyday, day-to day words that teachers are asking students to learn and use properly.

Calculating the number of words students are exposed to in elementary, middle, and high school is a complicated task. It often goes back to the definition of the word "word." In many cases, when calulating the number of words, researchers tend to use "word families," rather than individual words. This means that words such as "need, needed, needing, and needs" will be counted as one word. Also, multiple-meaning terms such as "check" are counted as one word, regardless of how many meanings it may have.

Teaching students independent word-learning strategies is critical for supporting vocabulary growth and development. Given the thousands of words students must learn to handle academic demands (Nagy & Anderson, 1984), direct instruction of vocabulary alone cannot shoulder the responsibility for increasing vocabulary knowledge. In fact, in their study of students in grades six through nine, Nagy and Anderson estimated that students in these grades may be exposed to 3,000 to 4,000 unfamiliar words, while reading close to one million words in context during each academic school year. These numbers indicate that students also need to acquire word-learning strategies for helping themselves figure out the meanings of words on their own (Graves, 2006).

Early vocabulary researchers reported figures ranging from 2,500 to 26,000 words in the vocabularies of typical grade 1 students and from 19,000 to 200,000 words for college graduate students (Beck & McKeown, 1991). As researchers began to define more clearly what they meant by vocabulary size, the estimates became more precise. At the present time, there is considerable consensus among researchers that students add approximately 2,000 to 3,500 distinct words yearly to their reading vocabularies (Anderson & Nagy, 1992; Anglin, 1993; Beck & McKeown, 1991; White et al., 1990).

Nagy and Anderson estimated that school texts from grades 3 through 9 contain approximately 88,500 distinct word families. Clearly, acquiring meanings for this many words is a formidable task.

Yet somehow, most students do steadily acquire a large number of new words each school year. To understand the magnitude of this accomplishment, consider what learning this number of words would require in terms of instruction. To directly teach students even 3,000 words a year would mean teaching approximately 17 words each school *day* (e.g., 3,000 words/180 school days). Estimates vary, but reviews of classroom intervention studies suggest that, in general, no more than eight to ten words can be taught effectively each week. This means no more than approximately 400 words can be taught in a year (Stahl & Fairbanks, 1986). Using a simple calculation, 3,000 − 400 = 2,600, produces the conclusion that students must find ways other than direct classroom instruction to learn words.

So how do students acquire so many new words? An extensive body of research indicates that the answer is through incidental learning—that is, through exposure to and interaction with increasingly complex and rich oral language and by encountering lots of new words in text, either through their own reading or by being read to (National Reading Panel, 2000). However, such incidental encounters cannot ensure that students will acquire in-depth meanings of specific words (Fukkink & de Glopper, 1998). For some words, such as those that are crucial for understanding a literature selection or a content area concept, most students need intentional and explicit instruction.

What Are the Multiple Levels of "Knowing" a Word?

As teachers create their lessons, it probably becomes clear that some vocabulary words on the lesson plan may be more important than other words. Some of the words may require an extensive, comprehensive understanding, whereas other words may need somewhat less understanding. This difference in "word understanding" translates into how much instructional time is needed to achieve the desired outcome. Generally, the more extensive the students' desired word understanding, the more instructional time is needed. For this reason, teachers must carefully scrutinize and prioritize their content vocabulary lists.

One of the easier methods used by many teachers is to use the Vocabulary Word Grid (see Tables 3.1 and 3.2). Teachers list their lesson's key vocabulary in the left-side column and then decide and check (X) which level of "knowing" the teacher expects of students. If "No Knowledge" is checked, the word should be removed from the lesson's key vocabulary word list.

Table 3.1 Vocabulary Word Grid

KEY VOCABULARY	NO KNOWLEDGE	GENERAL KNOWLEDGE	BASIC KNOWLEDGE	RICH KNOWLEDGE

Table 3.2 Sample of a Completed Vocabulary Word Grid.

KEY VOCABULARY	NO KNOWLEDGE	GENERAL KNOWLEDGE	BASIC KNOWLEDGE	RICH KNOWLEDGE
Vocabulary #1			X	
Vocabulary #2				X
Vocabulary #3		X		
Vocabulary #4			X	

Many teachers also like to conduct a Vocabulary Pre-Check (See Tables 3.3 and 3.4) with their students.

Another way teachers can conduct a vocabulary pre-check is by listing all the new or upcoming words on the board and asking each student to complete the Write-In Vocabulary Pre-Check Form. See an example in Table 3.5.

Table 3.3 Vocabulary Pre-Check

KEY VOCABULARY	THIS WORD IS TOTALLY NEW TO ME.	I'VE HEARD OR SEEN THIS WORD, BUT I'M NOT SURE WHAT IT MEANS.	I KNOW ONE DEFINITION OR COULD USE THIS WORD IN A SENTENCE.	I KNOW SEVERAL WAYS THIS WORD COULD BE USED.
Vocabulary #1				
Vocabulary #2				
Vocabulary #3				
Vocabulary #4				

Table 3.4 Sample Completed Vocabulary Pre-Check

KEY VOCABULARY	THIS WORD IS TOTALLY NEW TO ME.	I'VE HEARD OR SEEN THIS WORD, BUT I'M NOT SURE WHAT IT MEANS.	I KNOW ONE DEFINITION OR COULD USE THIS WORD IN A SENTENCE.	I KNOW SEVERAL WAYS THIS WORD COULD BE USED.
Vocabulary #1		X		
Vocabulary #2			X	
Vocabulary #3	X			
Vocabulary #4			X	

Table 3.5 Sample Completed Write-In Vocabualry Pre-Check

THIS WORD IS TOTALLY NEW TO ME.	I'VE HEARD OR SEEN THIS WORD, BUT I'M NOT SURE WHAT IT MEANS.	I KNOW ONE DEFINITION OR COULD USE THIS WORD IN A SENTENCE.	I KNOW SEVERAL WAYS THIS WORD COULD BE USED.
vector	toxin	infection	vaccine
antigen	bacteria	virus	
pathogen		immunity	
		antibody	

What about Multiple-Meaning Words?

Content key vocabulary words frequently have very different meanings, depending on how they are used in a sentence. Instructional practice in most classes should include strategies for students to determine the context (how the word is used in the sentence) in which a multiple-meaning word is used. Students should be taught how to look for contextual clues—before the word, after the word, the placement of the word in the sentence, or even within the word.

Many standardized tests assess words with multiple meanings in their vocabulary sections. Familiar, frequently used words tend to have more meanings than less frequent words. For example, one study found that 72 percent of the most frequently occurring 9,000 words contained multiple meanings (Johnson & Pearson, 1984). Other research has demonstrated the significance of context in acquiring and testing multiple-meaning words. Many factors contribute to the difficulty understanding these words, including context, a child's previous experience with the words in that context, and the degree of meaning overlap between the words' meanings (Johnson et al., 1997).

Homonyms are words having the same pronunciation but different meanings, origins, or spelling. Some homonyms have the same pronunciation, but different spelling (e.g., write/right, dough/doe, would/wood, do/dew/due, fore/four/for). These are called homophones. Another type of homonym, called a homograph, are two or more words having the same spelling but two or more different meanings (e.g., scale, plot). Sometimes the same spelling results in a different pronunciation (e.g., present/present, read/read, bow/bow).

Homonyms, both homophones and homographs, can be a difficult learning barrier and cause confusion—especially for many struggling learners.

Countless terms used in day-to-day instruction have multiple meanings, as illustrated in Blake's scenario in the Introduction section of this chapter. Unfortunately, many teachers, in a wide variety of disciplines, do not take the time to consider which instructional terms in their content area have multiple meanings. No subject area is immune. Consider the many common terms used in math, science, language arts, social studies, health, and technology that have multiple meanings. Can you think of some common multiple-meaning terms in your discipline?

Expanding a learner's academic language vocabulary knowledge requires moving beyond the highlighted words in a textbook to include words crucial to the conceptual understanding of a topic. Students need multiple opportunities to practice using these words orally and in print. Reading glossary definitions are not sufficient. Strategies such as word walls and semantic webs can help students organize the new words in meaningful ways. Other vocabulary techniques include demonstrations, illustrations, art projects, and letting students select specific vocabulary words to study (Short & Echevarria, 2005).

Teachers who have language learners in their classroom should also understand that some "non-English words" may have unexpected translations. For example: Author and speaker Maggie Stiefvater tells the story that, "aware that I'm allergic to preservatives, I kindly got someone to translate the phrase, 'I can only eat food without preservatives' into Italian. They warned me, however, as they taught me how to say it, that the Italian word for 'preservatives' is the same as the word for 'condom', so that I should be careful how I look when I say it." (Internet www.goodreads.com/quotes/244313)

Classroom instruction involving multiple-meaning terms should be strategically planned and organized. The first step for the teacher is to identify all multiple-meaning terms in the upcoming lesson. Every comprehensive lesson plan should include a specific section for identifying key vocabulary. As teachers list the key vocabulary of a specific lesson, they should identify every term in one (or more) of three specific ways:

1. Is the key vocabulary word a new (N) term?

   • Example: Epidemiology (N)

2. Is the key vocabulary term a review (R) term?

   • Example: Aphorism (R)

3. Is the key vocabulary term a multiple-meaning term (MM)?

- Example: Mean (N), (MM)

- In this example, the term "mean" is both a new (N) and a multiple-meaning (MM) term.

Many teachers find a simple three-column grid (Table 3.6) helpful when planning for multiple-meaning vocabulary instruction. Teachers are encouraged to list and determine which of the lesson's key vocabulary words are unique or have multiple meanings. A blank template (T3.1) for this step is located at the end of this chapter.

When instruction involves a multiple-meaning word, teachers are encouraged to inform students that this key vocabulary word has another definition—or several other definitions. Teachers should share (or ask students to share) at least one other definition and indicate a possible course or place where students might see or hear this "other" definition.

Understanding that the language proficiency range of students in U.S. K–12 schools is enormous, the tables that follow (See Tables 3.7–3.10) offer a place to start when preparing instructional lessons. However, the classroom teacher will know best which words are most appropriate for his or her students.

Table 3.6 Multiple-Meaning Grid: Science Example

KEY VOCABULARY WORD	MULTIPLE MEANINGS?	CLASS MEANING	ANOTHER DEFINITION
Plot	√	To determine the location of (a point) by means of its coordinates	A small piece of land
Scale	√	Outer covering of many fishes, snakes, and lizards	An instrument for weighing
Quotient		A division answer	– – – –
Check	√	To examine something to discover facts or prove true or right	A written order directing a bank to pay money
Degree	√	A unit for measuring the opening of an angle	A unit for measuring temperature

Table 3.7 Basic Level Multiple-Meaning Words

bat	can	face	fall	foot
light	mean	ring	rock	run
saw	star	stick	top	trip

Table 3.8 Elementary Level Multiple-Meaning Words

back	bowl	bank	bark	board
brush	check	clear	degree	draw
drill	freeze	head	key	letter
right	present	rose	safe	second
spring	state	table	watch	wave

Table 3.9 Middle School Level Multiple-Meaning Words

against	act	angle	batter	cast
chair	charge	coast	court	current
crane	date	draft	fuse	interest
judge	marker	organ	party	plane
screen	shock	speaker	suit	tip

Table 3.10 High School Level Multiple-Meaning Words

blunt	base	coach	coast	crop
custom	doctor	figure	firm	grave
harbor	hatch	interest	issue	lean
lounge	market	page	palm	pitch
prune	reservation	spare	solution	sentence

What about Prefixes, Suffixes, and Roots?

Prefixes, suffixes, and roots are an extremely important part of vocabulary development. Often, specific content areas have some common core prefixes, suffixes, and roots.

Prefix—A prefix is a syllable, syllables, or word put at the beginning of a word to change its meaning or to make another word. The actual word "prefix" is a good example: "pre" means "before," and "fix" means "to fasten or attach." Thus, prefix literally means "something attached to the beginning of something." For example, *dis-* in disorient is a prefix. The health education field has many common prefixes that are often used in instructional topics. Some examples include: *cardio-, mal-, hemo-, hydro-, derm-, therm-, quad-, leuko-,* or *psycho-*. The good news for teachers is a fairly small number of prefixes is used in a large number of words. Indeed, nine prefixes account for 75 percent of words with prefixes (White, Sowell, & Yanagihara, 1989). Those prefixes are:

un-	dis-	in- (in)
re-	en-, em-	over-
in- (not)	non-	mis-

Suffix—A suffix is a syllable or syllables put at the end of a word to change its meaning or to make another word. For example, -itis in tonsillitis is a suffix. Other examples include: -ectomy, -rrhea, -meter, -oma, -osis, or -ology. Some of the most common suffixes include:

-acy	-ism	-ship	-ize
-al	-ist	-sion, -tion	-able
-ance, -ence	-ity	-ate	-ful
-dom	-ment	-en	-ious
-er	-ness	-ify	-less

Root word—A word from which other words are made: e.g *Room* is the root of *roominess, roomer, roommate,* and *roomy.* Sometimes a root word is called a base word. Some common root words include:

bio	magni	chrono
cede	mono	dict
geo	script	phil
hydro	thermo	photo

Teachers should take the time to specifically teach their contentcommon prefixes, suffixes, and root words—especially those that are basic and common to the discipline and will likely reoccur in subsequent lessons.

What Are Some Basic Vocabulary Teaching Strategies and Learning Activities?

First, we need to clarify the terms "teaching strategies" and "learning activities." These two terms are entirely different—even though some teachers mistakenly use them interchangeably. "Teaching strategies" refers to the sructure, system, methods, techniques, procedures, and processses that a teacher uses during instruction. These are strategies the *teacher* employs to assist student learning. Learning activities refer to the teacher-guided instructional tasks or assignments for students. These are *student* activities (Wandberg & Rohwer, 2010).

One of the more common vocabulary instructional practice is the use of word play. Word play consists of addressing words through games, rhymes, tongue twisters, or any method employed to increase students' awareness of the meaning and value of individual words. Simple teaching strategies and learning activities for vocabulary support often copy many common games such as:

- Jeopardy!

- Concentration

- Matching (words to icons or definitions)

- Triple column matches

- Bingo

- Crossword puzzles

- Flashcards

- Writing silly sentences

- Word search

- Word challenges

- Password

- Roll-the-dice words

Word walls consist of words posted on classroom walls as a means of immersing students in language. (See Figure 3.1). To help students learn and remember the important content words, teachers often put a drawing, icon, or pictograph next to the word.

In classrooms with little or no wall space, teachers often put their word walls on the ceiling. Of course, this leads teachers to the clever remark, "If you don't know the word, look it UP" while gazing up at the ceiling. Teachers and students add new words as they come in contact with them. Word walls can be used to teach vocabulary, pronunciation, word families, categorization, and spelling.

Some teachers find it advantageous to separate their classroom word walls into two or more sections, with one section devoted specifically to key vocabulary terms with multiple meanings or similar prefixes, suffixes, and roots. Teachers often use multiple-meaning pictograph word walls, rather than written definitions. In this context, the pictograph is a picture, drawing, icon, sign, or symbol illustrating two or more meanings for the multiple-meaning words. See Figure 3.3 for an example of a pictograph web.

Figure 3.1 Sample Word Wall

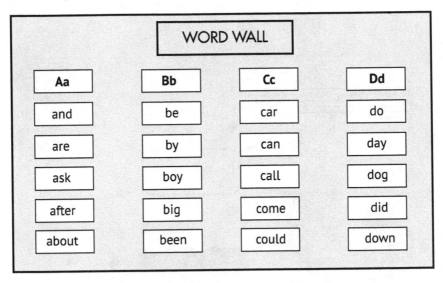

A graphic organizer (see Chapter 4 for more detailed information) is another instructional strategy that can help students learn multiple-meaning words. For example, a simple web (see Figure 3.2) can be used to illustrate more than one definition of a word. A blank template (T3.2) is located at the end of this chapter.

For some students, it may be advantageous to use pictures, drawings, or clipart to illustrate the various definitions of a multiple-meaning word. Similar to the definition web, a pictograph web (Figure 3.2) simply has icons instead of definitions. A blank template (T3.3) is located at the end of this chapter.

Many times, it may be best to allow students to create (draw) their own icons at the end of each line, thereby creating their own personalized pictograph for that multiple-meaning word.

Figure 3.2 Multiple-Meaning Definition Web

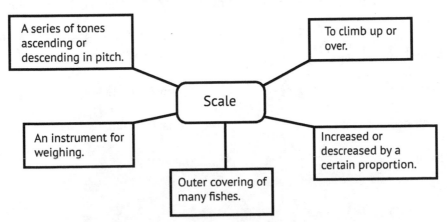

Figure 3.3 Multiple-Meaning Pictograph Web

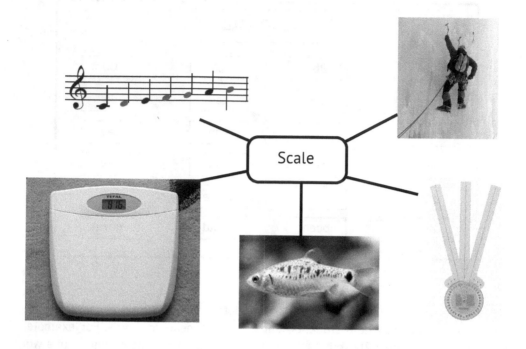

Other common vocabulary strategies include using the Frayer Model, alphalaries, and prediction charts.

Frayer Model

The Frayer Model (see Figure 3.4) is a type of graphic organizer, designed by Dorothy Frayer and her colleagues at the University of Wisconsin, to provide for a thorough understanding of new words. The Frayer Model is essentially a vocabulary development tool. The foursquare model provides an opportunity for students to examine and analyze a word from four various aspects. A teacher should choose the most appropriate four aspects based on the word and the level of the students. The most commonly used aspects include:

- Definition
- Fact
- Sentence
- Icon

- Example
- Non-Example
- Characteristic
- Drawing

Figure 3.4 Blank Frayer Model

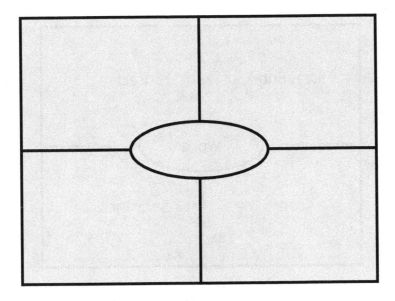

Any combination of appropriate word aspects can be selected. Figures 3.5 and 3.6 are two examples of the many possibilities.

Figure 3.5 Frayer Model, Example 1

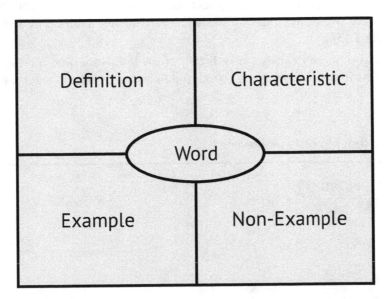

Figure 3. 6 Frayer Model, Example 2

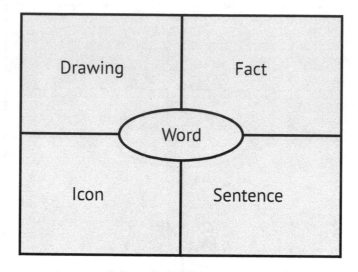

The Frayer Model is designed to provide students with a deeper and more comprehensive understanding of an important instructional word. As illustrated, some Frayer Models are designed for students to identify what the word (or concept) is, but also what it is not. Teachers often have students create Frayer Model dictionaries by having several Frayer Models on each side of several pieces of paper.

Alphalary

The word "alphalary" is a combination of two words—alphabet and vocabulary. Alphalaries are tools to help students organize key vocabulary words in a specific content, unit, or theme. There are two main types of alphalaries: vertical (see Tables 3.11 and 3.12) and grid (see Table 3.13).

The vertical alphalary consists of a listing of 26 lines—one line for each letter of the alphabet. As important words are introduced in lessons, students enter them in their alphalary.

Table 3.11 Vertical Alphalary (Abbreviated)

LETTER	WORD(S)
A	
B	
C	
D	
E ↓	

Table 3.12 Sample Vertical Alphalary (Abbreviated)

LETTER	WORD(S)
A	alcohol, addiction, abuse
B	barbiturates, blackout
C	carbon monoxide, carcinogen
D	drug, dendrite, dependence
E ↓	ethanol

The grid alphalary is composed of a 5 × 5 grid consisting of 25 boxes. See Table 3.13.

Table 3.13 Blank Grid Alphalary

A	B	C	D	E
F	G	H	I	J
K	L	M	N	O
P	Q	R	S	T
U	V	W	X	Y/Z

As indicated previously, when important words are introduced in lessons, students enter them in their grid alphalary. See Table 3.14.

The grid alphalary easily lends itself to bingo-like games that many teachers employ for vocabulary review lessons.

(Continued)

Table 3.14 Sample Grid Alphalary

A	B	C	D	E
Absorb	BMR	Calorie	Daily values	Edema
Acid	Beriberi	Carbohydrate	Dehydration	Electrolytes
Additives	Bile	Carcinogen	Diabetes	Enriched
Allergy	Biotin	Cell	Diet	Enzymes
Amino acids	Bladder	Cholestrol	Digest	
Anemia	Botulism	Colon	Dysentery	
F	**G**	**H**	**I**	**J**
Famine	Genes	Heartburn	Immunity	Jaundice
Fat-free	Germ	Hemoglobin	Insoluble	
	Glucose		Insulin	
	Grams		Ions	
K	**L**	**M**	**N**	**O**
Keratin	Lactase	Malnutrition	Natural foods	Obesity
Ketone	Lactose	Melatonin	Niacin	IOLsOrganic
Kidneys	Lean	Metabolism	Nutrients	Oxidation
	Legumes	Minerals		
	Lipid			
P	**Q**	**R**	**S**	**T**
Pancreas	Quackery	RDA	Salts	Thiamin
Pasteurization		Refined	Sanitation	Tofu
pH		Retinol	Solvent	Toxicity
Phenykletonuria		Riboflavin	Starch	Triglycerides
		Rickets	Sugars	
U	**V**	**W**	**X**	**Y/Z**
Ulcer	Vegan	Wasting	Xerophthalmia	Zygote
Urea	Vegetarians	Wean		Zoochemicals
	Vitamins	Whole grain		

Vocabulary Prediction Chart

A Vocabulary Prediction Chart (see Tables 3.15 to 3.17) is most commonly used for the very important words in a lesson. Its purpose is to allow students to think about and ponder the meaning of a word, or words, in an upcoming reading, often based on some teacher-given clues.

Example:

Step 1: The teacher hands out, or has students make, a vocabulary prediction chart. See Table 3.15

Table 3.15 Blank Vocabulary Prediction Chart

WORD	PREDICTED MEANING	AFTER-READING MEANING

Step 2: The teacher might say:

> In a few minutes, you will be reading some information about the Great Lakes. One of the words in the reading is "seiche." Please add this word to your vocabulary prediction chart and predict the meaning of "seiche."

At that point, each student adds the key vocabulary word to his or her prediction chart. Then, based on the teacher's clue (e.g., Great Lakes), the student predicts the meaning of the key vocabulary word. See Table 3.16

Table 3.16 Partially Completed Vocabulary Prediction Chart

WORD	PREDICTED MEANING	AFTER-READING MEANING
seiche	A type of shoreline rock	

Step 3: At this point, some teachers ask students to share their predicted meanings—and why they predicted that meaning—to either the entire class, to a partner, or to a small group.

Step: 4: The students now read the information. As an example, the reading might be:

> The Great Lakes aren't large enough to generate the immense wall of water associated with tsunamis, which may reach as high as 100 feet at the coast, traveling 20–40 mph. The Great Lakes are subject to a large wave called a seiche (pronounced saysh), more likely caused by a storm front accompanied by high winds and sudden change in air pressure. An earthquake can also cause a seiche.

Step 5: As a final step, the students write the correct definition in their Vocabulary Prediction Chart.

Table 3.17 Sample Completed Vocabulary Prediction Chart

WORD	PREDICTED MEANING	AFTER-READING MEANING
seiche	A type of shoreline rock	A large wave

The Frayer Model, alphalaries, and prediction charts are examples of common vocabulary teaching strategies. There are many others. Each strategy has its strengths and limitations. Some strategies may be more appropriate when teachers change rooms frequently, or for certain struggling students, or for the degree to which the teacher wants the student to "know" the key vocabulary word.

The English language, as with many other languages, can be difficult to learn. Look at these statements, and put yourself in the mind-set of a student who struggles with the English language.

1. The bandage was wound around the wound.

2. The farm was used to produce produce.

3. The dump was so full that it had to refuse more refuse.

4. We must polish the Polish furniture.

5. He could lead if he would get the lead out.

6. The soldier decided to desert his dessert in the desert.

7. Since there is no time like the present, I decided to present the present today.

8. They were too close to the door to close it.

9.   The insurance was invalid for the invalid.

10. I did not object to the object.

11. Lead poisoning can lead to health issues.

12. Does the deer see the does?

13. The dove dove down to its nest.

14. I drove down the windy road on a windy day.

Hopefully, now, as teachers, you can more clearly understand why many struggling learners have a challenging road ahead when they are expected to learn academic content and English simultaneously.

SUMMARY

Many researchers and teachers believe that vocabulary is one of the best, if not the best, predictors of academic learning, achievement, and success. Therefore, teachers are asked to spend a good portion of their instructional time devoted to vocabulary development. Multiple-meaning terms, prefixes, suffixes, and root words can be a learning barrier to many students. There are several effective vocabualry strategies and learning activities that teachers can draw on to reduce the barriers associated with vocabulary development. They include formal vocabulary strategies, the extensive use of visuals, and word walls, as well as individual, partner, and small group activities and competitive games.

REVIEW

1.   What is the difference between a homophone and a homograph? Give an example of each.

2.   How can teachers be prepared for upcoming lessons involving multiple-meaning terms?

3.   What are three commonly used multiple-meaning terms in your content or discipline?

4.   What are two instructional strategies teachers can use to help students learn key vocabulary words that are multiple-meaning terms?

5.   Complete the five templates at the end of this chapter.

REFERENCES

Anderson, R. C., & Freebody, P. (1981). Vocabulary knowledge. In J. Guthrie (Ed.), *Comprehension and teaching: Research reviews* (pp. 77–117). Newark, DE: International Reading Association.

Baumann, J. F., Kame'enui, E. J., & Ash, G. E. (2003). Research on vocabulary instruction: Voltaire redux. In J. Flood, D. Lapp, J. R. Squire, & J. M. Jensen (Eds.), *Handbook on research on teaching the English language arts* (2nd ed., pp. 752–785). Mahwah, NJ: Erlbaum.

Becker, W. C. (1977). Teaching reading and language to the disadvantaged—What we have learned from field research. *Harvard Educational Review, 47*, 518–543.

Davis, F. B. (1968). "Research on Comprehension in Reading." *Reading Research Quarterly, 3*, 499–545.

Davis, F. B. (1944). "Fundamental Factors in Reading Comprehension." *Psychometrika 9*, 185–97.

Fukkink, R. G., & de Glopper, K. (1998). Effects of instruction in deriving word meaning from context: A meta-analysis. *Review of Educational Research, 68*(4), 450–469.

Graves, M. F. (2006). *The vocabulary book: Learning and instruction.* Newark, DE: International Reading Association.

Graves, M. F. (2009). *Teaching individual words* (p. 11). The Practitioner's Bookshelf.

Harmon, J. M., Wood, K. W., & Hedrick, W. B. (in press). Vocabulary instruction in middle and secondary content classrooms: Understandings and directions from research. In A. Farstrup & J. Samuels (Eds.), *What research has to say about vocabulary instruction.* Newark, DE: International Reading Association.

Johnson, C. (1997). Assessing children's knowledge of multiple meaning words. *American Journal of Speech-Language Pathology,* vol. 6, 77–86.

Johnson, D. D., & Pearson, P. D. (1984). *Teaching reading vocabulary* (2nd Edition). New York: Holt, Rinehart & Winston.

Nagy, W. E., & Anderson, R. C. (1984). How many words are there in printed school English? *Reading Research Quarterly, 19*, 304–330.

National Reading Panel (2000). www.nationalreadingpanel.org/publications/publications.htm (Retrived March 2013.)

Reutzel, D. Ray (2004). *The essentials of teaching children to read.* Prentice Hall.

Short, D., and Echevarria, J. (2005). Teacher skills to support English language learners. *Educational Leadership,* pp. 8–13; 6 pages.

Stanovich, K. (1986). Matthew effects in reading: Some consequences of individual differences in the acquisition of literacy. *Reading Research Quarterly.* Fall 1986, XXI/4.

Stiefvater, M. Internet. www.goodreads.com/quotes/244313 (Retrieved March 2013.)

Wandberg, R., and Rohwer, J. (2010). *Teaching health education in language diverse classrooms.* Sudbury, MA: Jones and Bartlett, Publishers.

Whipple, G. (Ed.). (1925). *The twenty-fourth yearbook of the National Society for the Study of Education: Report of the National Committee on Reading.* Bloomington, IL: Public School Publishing.

White, G., Sowell, J., & Yanagihara, A. Teaching Elementary Students to Use Word-Part Clues. www.books.google.com/books?id=MKT_2CD2rVQC&pg=PA83&lpg=PA83&dq (Retrived March 2013.)

FIGURE SOURCES

TEMPLATE 3.1: IDENTIFYING MULTIPLE-MEANING WORDS

Step 1: Select a grade, course, and unit of your choice

Step 2: In column 1, list the key vocabulary words aligned with your grade, course, and unit.

Step 3: In column 2, check the words that have multiple meanings

Step 4: In column 3, write the definition of all words that will be used in class for this lesson.

Step 5: In column 4, write at least one OTHER definition of the multiple-meaning words that students might encounter in other classes or elsewhere.

Grade: _____

Course: _____

Unit: _____

KEY VOCABULARY WORDS	MULTIPLE MEANINGS?	CLASS MEANING	ANOTHER DEFINITION

TEMPLATE 3.2: MULTIPLE-MEANING WORD WEB

Step 1: Select a grade, course, and unit of your choice
Step 2: Write a multiple meaning word aligned with your selected grade, course, and unit in the center oval.
Step 3: In the outer ovals write other definitions of the center word that occur in other subject areas or elsewhere.

Grade: _____
Course: _____
Unit: _____

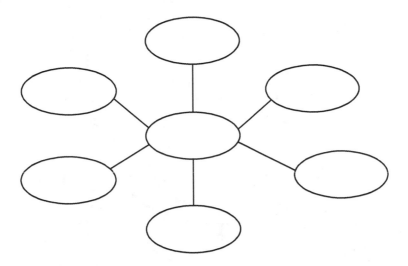

TEMPLATE 3.3: MULTIPLE-MEANING PICTOGRAPH WEB

Step 1: Select a grade, course, and unit of your choice
Step 2: Write a multiple meaning word, as defined by your grade, course, and unit in the center oval.
Step 3: At the end of the lines illustrate, by pictures, drawings, or icons, the various definitions of the center word.

Grade: _____
Course: _____
Unit: _____

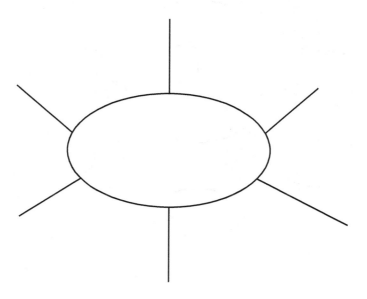

TEMPLATE 3.4: FRAYER MODEL

Step 1: Select a grade, course, and unit of your choice

Step 2: Select two key vocabulary words associated with your selected grade, course, and unit. Write the key vocabulary words in the center oval of each Frayer Model below.

Step 3: Select the four most appropriate terms (definition, fact, sentence, icon, example, non-example, characteristic, or drawing) that will help students learn the key vocabulary words.

Grade: _____

Course: _____

Unit: _____

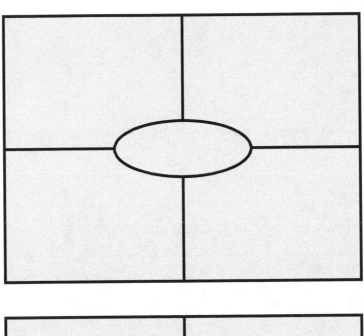

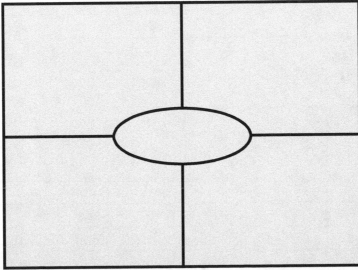

TEMPLATE 3.5: VERTICAL ALPHALARY

Step 1: Select a grade, course, and unit of your choice
Step 2: Complete the vertical alphalary with terms from your selected grade, course, and unit.
Step 3: Circle the words that are multiple-meaning words.

Grade: _____
Course: _____
Unit: _____

LETTER	WORD(S)
A	
B	
C	
D	
E	
F	
G	
H	
I	
J	
K	
L	
M	
N	
O	
P	
Q	
R	
S	
T	
U	
V	
W	
X	
Y	
Z	

Chapter four

VISUAL REPRESENTATIONS

Education is not filling a pail but the lighting of a fire.

—WILLIAM BUTLER YEATS

OBJECTIVES

Readers will be able to:

1. Create and implement a variety of appropriate nonlinguistic teaching strategies and learning activities.

2. Demonstrate how to create nonlinguistic strategies and activities.

3. Cite several benefits of, and reasons for, using visual representations.

4. Explain several types of graphic organizers.

5. Explain the steps in constructing a graphic organizer.

KEY VOCABULARY

Readers will be able to define or describe each term in the context of the chapter information.

Body Map	Rubric	Venn Diagram
Continuum Scale	Sequence Map	Visual Representation
Graphic Organizer	Spider Map	Web Map
Nonlinguistic	T-Chart	

INTRODUCTION

Using visual representations to represent a word, idea, sound, or image is not a new approach to teaching. Pictures, characters, and symbols have been used for thousands of years. One of the most common historical examples of visual representations is the early writings of the Egyptians about 5000 years ago. The Egyptian writing called hieroglyphics (visual representations) used pictures to represent different objects, actions, sound or ideas. There were more than 700 hieroglyphs. Some hieroglyphs were read right to left, some left to right and some top to bottom. Likewise, today's instructional practices use various visual representations that may or may not relay the message in a common reading form—left to right.

Visual learners make up approximately 65 percent of the student population. Auditory learners comprise approximately 30 percent of the student population. About five percent of the student population are kinesthetic learners (MindWorks 2013). With these percentages in mind, using visual representations as an integral part of instruction will allow teachers to reach far more students. This is not to say that teachers should abandon all auditory and kinesthetic instructional practices. Many auditory and kinesthetic instructional practices can—and should—incorporate visual representations.

The Visual Teaching Alliance (2013) reports several facts related to visual learners, including:

- The brain processes visual information 60,000 times faster than text.

- 90 percent of information coming in to the brain is visual.

- 40 percent of all nerve fibers connected to the brain are linked to the retina.

- Our eyes can register 36,000 visual messages per hour.

- Visual aids in the classroom improve learning by up to 400 percent.

Visual learners often have difficulty with oral directions, especially those with more than two steps. They learn best when the assignment is demonstrated or illustrated, rather than given orally. They have difficulty following lectures (especially when there are no visual clues). Visual learners have trouble remembering information given orally without being able to see it. In the classroom, the visual learner may appear to "zone out" during lengthy oral presentations.

What Are Visual Representations?

One way teachers can enhance and extend student learning is through the use of visual representations, sometimes called nonlinguistic representations. Visual representations come in a variety of formats and have been extensively researched for their effectiveness in supporting and improving student learning, success, and achievement. Visual representations allow students to create visual or symbolic representations of what they hear or read. Through visual representations, students are able to convey important content facts, concepts, and vocabulary. For many teachers, a graphic organizer (sometimes called a mind map, concept map, or web) is the most commonly used visual representation. Other visual representations include photos, technology, games, bulletin boards, role playing, models, sculptures, paintings, dioramas, costumes, drawings, and icons. The use of visual representations for a variety of students is well researched as an effective practice. Visual representations can be effectively used in a wide range of academic disciplines, including math, science, health, language arts, social studies, art, and music. This chapter provides the reader with multiple methods and templates to incorporate visual representation practices in all content areas.

What Are Graphic Organizers?

Visual representations are especially important in language and ability in diverse education settings and classrooms. One type of visual representation is commonly referred to as a graphic organizer. A graphic organizer is simply a visual representation of facts, information, concepts, and/or skills and how they are—or are not—linked together. All age and grade levels of learners benefit from the use of graphic organizers, and these visual representations have applications in many different content areas (Dye, 2000). Learners must have information presented in a clear, concise, and organized form if they are to make progress in content area classrooms.

Graphic organizers have great potential for students with learning disabilities (Gagnon & Maccini, 2000). The facts and concepts, in purely linguistic form, in today's classrooms are often overwhelming to struggling learners. Transposing that information into a visual representation can enhance the learning, comprehension, and recall. Fountas and Pinnell (2001) cite that when content is illustrated with diagrams, students can maintain the information over a longer period of time.

Graphic organizers portray knowledge in a meaningful way. This helps bring clarity to ideas as connections (and disconnections) are made. Difficult concepts can be simplified and arranged so that the visual representation of content is organized and meaningful. Using a graphic organizer to link newly learned information to an existing knowledge base is a viable strategy for teachers and students. Linking new information to past learning seems to be precisely what students need in order for learning to result (U.S. Department of Education, 1987).

What Are the Reasons for, and the Benefits of, Graphic Organizers?

The dual-coding theory suggests that knowledge is stored in the brain in two forms—linguistic and nonlinguistic (or imagery). The linguistic form consists of words, phrases, and statements. The nonlinguistic (or imagery) form consists of mental pictures such as photos, drawings, arrows, and symbols.

Under the auspices of Inspiration Software, Inc., the Institute for the Advancement of Research in Education (IARE) provides educators with evidence of the instructional effectiveness of the use of graphic organizers. Using the definitions set forth by Section 9101 of the *No Child Left Behind Act (NCLB)* of 2001, IARE selected 29 scientifically based research studies that applied rigorous, systematic, and objective procedures to obtain reliable and valid knowledge relevant to education activities and programs.

Scientifically based research cited in the literature review demonstrates that a research base exists to support the use of graphic organizers for improving student learning and performance across grade levels, with diverse students, and in a broad range of content areas. IARE conclusions from this review include:

1. Reading comprehension: The use of graphic organizers is effective in improving students' reading comprehension.

2. Student achievement: Students using graphic organizers show achievement benefits across content areas and grade levels. Achievement benefits are also seen with students with learning disabilities.

3. Thinking and learning skills: The process of developing and using a graphic organizer enhances skills such as developing and organizing ideas, seeing relationships, and categorizing concepts.

4. Retention: The use of graphic organizers aids students in retention and recall of information.

5. Cognitive learning theory: The use of graphic organizers supports implementation of cognitive learning theories: dual-coding theory, schema theory, and cognitive load theory.

The dual-coding theory recommends that classroom teachers use both forms in their instruction. The more that both forms—linguistic and nonlinguistic—are presented, the more students are able to comprehend and recall information. It has even been shown that explicitly engaging students in the creation of nonlinguistic representations stimulates and increases activity in the brain (Gerlic & Jausovec, 1999).

Teachers report many student benefits for using graphic organizers. These include:

1. improved social skills.

2. improved process-oriented and strategic learning.

3. improved questioning ability.

4. improved reflection and decision making.

5. improved critical thinking.

6. improved attitude toward learning.

7. improved ability to organize thinking.

8. improved understanding of the different ways to represent and view information.

9. improved understanding and retention of content.

Teachers, especially those working with struggling students, have identified several reasons for their fondness of graphic organizers. These reasons include:

1. Once students learn to use graphic organizers, they often start to use them spontaneously and independently.

2. Graphic organizers help timid or reluctant students make oral presentations.

3. Graphic organizers help students remember important information.

4. Graphic organizers are excellent tools to help a small group of students stay focused on the task.

5. Graphic organizers help students translate often complex or confusing textbook information into meaningful understandings.

6. Graphic organizers help students gather and organize information.

When Can Graphic Organizers Be Used?

One of the great advantages of using graphic organizers in the classroom is the relatively low cost compared to some of the newer, more costly technological instructional tools, mechanisms, and materials. Students can be asked to replicate—in their notebooks—a graphic organizer that the teacher has drawn on the board. Graphic organizers can support a lesson and be used at most any time throughout a lesson, such as during warm-up activities, direct teaching, student performance, and class review.

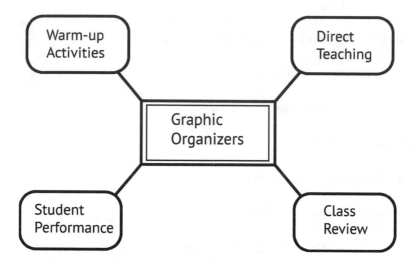

Graphic organizers can be used during warm-up activities:

- to focus students on the learner objectives

- to generate ideas

- as a pre-assessment to determine the background knowledge or skill of students on a particular subject or concept.

Graphic organizers can be used to enhance student learning during the direct teaching phase, as part of:

- demonstrations

- lectures

- guest speakers

- multimedia presentations.

One of the most powerful lesson sections to use graphic organizers is during the student performance phase. This phase consists of high student engagement, such as:

- individual, partner, and small group work

- student presentations, debates, point/counterpoints

- student creations, research, advocacy, inventions, discovery, mutimedia

- student inquiry, analysis, assessment, evaluation

- student skill development—problem solving and decision making

And finally, graphic organizers can be effectively used at the end of class during class review:

- to provide a formative assessment of individual and team work progress

- during active questioning of the lesson's objectives

- for student pairing and sharing

- to summarize lesson objectives

- to review notes.

Graphic organizers can easily be differentiated to better accommodate student needs and proficiencies. Partitially completed graphic organizers is one of the more common ways teachers differentiate graphic organizers for their struggling students. Student learning, especially those who struggle with language, can be enhanced by working with graphic organizers in small groups. This format will often expose the student(s) to all four language domains—reading, writing, listening, and speaking.

How Can Teachers Help Students Construct Graphic Organizers?

Teachers are not the only ones who should be making graphic organizers. The construction of graphic organizers should gradually move from the teacher to the students (see

Figure 4.1

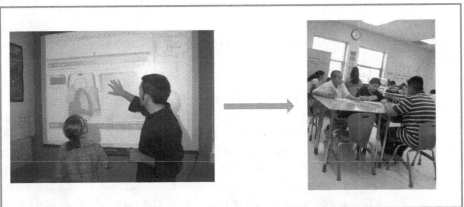

Figure 4.1). Early on, students should be exposed to the various types and formats of graphic organizers. Many teachers—elementary through high school level—have sample graphic organizers permanently displayed in their classrooms throughout the school year.

However, before expecting students to create graphic organizers teachers should:

1. Demonstrate the use and construction of graphic organizers.

2. Give students partially constructed graphic organizers.

3. Remember to scaffold the instructional process by gradually withdrawing instructional support. Two common scaffolding techniques are:

    a. Direct instruction > modeling > practice > independence

    b. Whole class > small group > partners > individual

Another way to help students create their own graphic organizers is to give them some step-by-step construction guidelines. Examples of construction guidelines include:

1. Identifying the main ideas, sections, or content.

2. Cluster or group words and ideas that are related.

3. Determining relationships (e.g., cause and effect, sequential, chronological)

4. Determining the type of graphic organizer that is most appropriate for the material and purpose.

5. Arranging ideas and drawing connecting lines.

6. Remember: There are many ways to visually represent ideas; change the type of graphic organizer, if desired.

7. Using icons and pictures, as well as words, in your graphic organizer.

8. When possible, using a variety of colors to represent different aspects of your graphic organizer.

Teachers often struggle with effective grading strategies for visual representations—especially when they are created by a small team of students. Teachers who create rubrics (see Chapter 8) for students based on specific visual representation criteria typically have the best grading success. Rubrics are a grading gradation tool for student work. Rubrics articulate gradations of quality. Rubrics are also good tools for individual self-assessment and peer assessment. Rubrics are often in a grid format (see Table 4.1). The left-side column lists the important grading criteria. The columns to the right of the criteria contain

Table 4.1 Sample Rubric Format

CRITERIA ↓	OUTSTANDING	PROFICIENT	BASIC	UNACCEPTABLE

the gradations of quality work. There are many possible "names" for these gradations. A common four-point gradation is outstanding, proficient, basic, and unacceptable. These columns often have a number associated with each gradation for scoring

Depending on the nature of the visual representation, some possible grading criteria include:

a. accuracy of information;

b. spelling and grammar;

c. completion of information;

d. information is clear (easy to interpret);

e. information is neat and presentable;

f. use of diagrams and illustrations;

g. size;

h. appropriate vocabulary;

i. student can verbally explain your graphic organizer to others;

j. author(s) names are included;

k. multiple colors were used;

l. product was completed on time.

In addition to the rubric, student self-assessments can be administered to visual representations completed by a team of students. See Table 4.2 for a basic example.

Table 4.2 Visual Representation Self-Assessment (4 high, 3, 2, 1 low)

ASSESSMENT ITEMS	4	3	2	1
We understood our task				
We stayed on the task				
Everyone contributed				
Everyone listened when others were speaking				
Everyone spoke and gave opinions				
We finished our task				
We followed the assignment rubric				

What Are the Common Types of Graphic Organizers?

Graphic organizers come in a multitude of sizes, shapes, and formats. Generally, they are designed to organize basic categories of information. These categories include:

- Sequence or time

- Cause and effect

- Compare and contrast

- Body spatial relationship

- Concept

- Descriptive

A brief list and description of the most common graphic organizers include:

1. A **concept** or **web map** (Figure 4.2) works well for mapping generic information, but particularly well for activating and mapping prior knowledge, brainstorming ideas, and gathering information from print or visual materials. They are also used to look at various definitions or examples of categories and characteristics.

2. When the information relating to a main idea or theme does not fit into a hierarchy, a **spider map** (Figure 4.3) can help with organization. The spider map is often used to connect specific details to a main concept or idea, such as in a story, article, or discussion.

Figure 4.2 Concept or Web Map

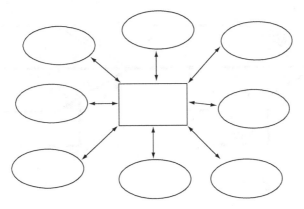

Figure 4.3 Spider Map

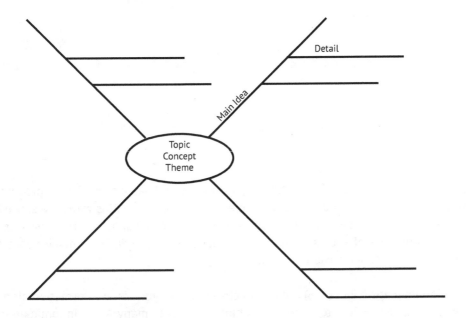

3. When information contains cause-and-effect problems and possible solutions, a **fishbone map** and a **cause-effect map** (Figure 4.4a, 4.4b) can be useful for organizing and visualizing various influences on specific events and are designed to show how certain events affect an outcome(s). Additional rectangles can be easily added to the fishbone map if multiple effects and/or solutions are generated. In some instances, students can visualize how one cause has one effect, how one cause can have multiple effects, or how multiple causes can have one or more effects.

Figure 4.4a Fishbone Map

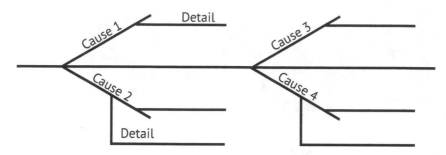

Figure 4.4b Cause-Effect Map

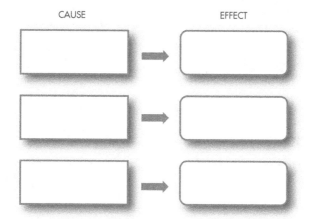

4. A **decision-making map** (Figure 4.5) helps students in the decision-making process or to compare different solutions to a problem. The map below illustrates the space for three possible alternatives to the question or problem and space for the positives (+) and negatives (–) of each alternative. Students can use the decision-making map for real-life or fictional decision making.

5. **Continuum maps** (Figure 4.6) are an effective way for organizing information along a dimension, such as less to more, low to high, and few to many. A continuum map may also be used to illustrate, for example, a time line of important dates in the history of an important event or topic.

6. A **cycle map** (Figure 4.7) is useful for organizing information that is circular or cyclical, with no absolute beginning or ending. Example: rain cycle or seasons cycle.

7. A **body map** (Figure 4.8) is one instructional option when dealing with various health-related issues, such as how or where various diseases affect the body, basic anatomy, or the effects of hypothermia. Body maps are also used as character maps to help students better understand another person's behaviors, feelings, or emotions.

Figure 4.5 Decision-Making Map

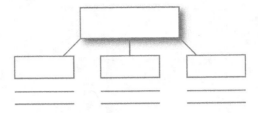

Figure 4.6 Continuum Map

Figure 4.7 Cycle Map

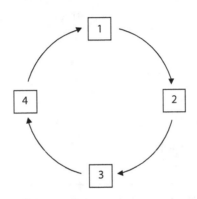

Figure 4.8 Body Map

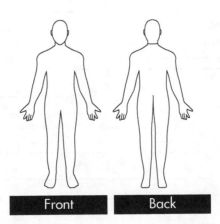

Figure 4.9 Compare-Contrast Map

ITEMS ➞			
ATTRIBUTE 1			
ATTRIBUTE 2			
ATTRIBUTE 3			

8. **Compare-contrast maps** (Figure 4.9) are used to compare and/or contrast two or more items based on similar attributes. For example, comparing-contrasting three U.S. states in terms of their selected attributes, such as topography, population, and temperature.

9. **Sequence maps** (Figure 4.10) allow students to organize sequential information. This could be a sequence of events or steps in a process. Examples include order of presidential succession, steps in solving math problems, or the order of the steps in cardiopulmonary resuscitation (CPR).

Figure 4.10 Sequence Chart

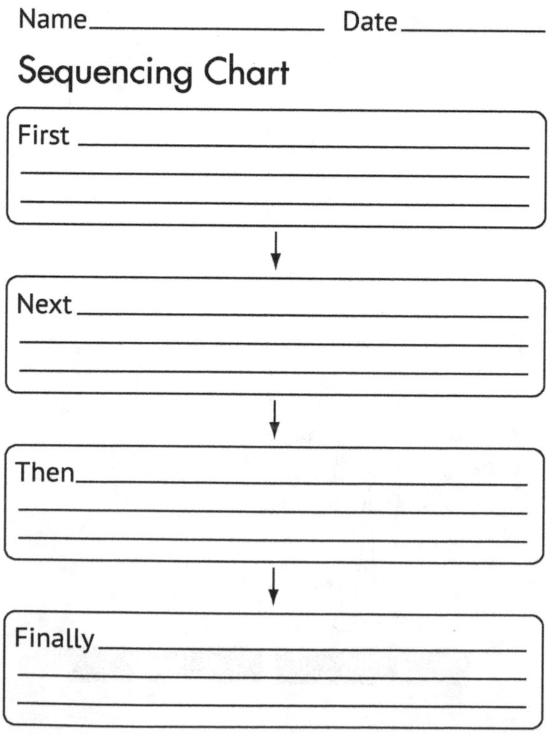

Name_____ Date_____

Sequencing Chart

First _____
_____
_____

↓

Next_____
_____
_____

↓

Then_____
_____
_____

↓

Finally_____
_____
_____

Figure 4.11a Double Venn Diagram

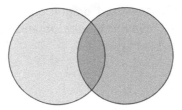

Figure 4.11b Triple Venn Diagram

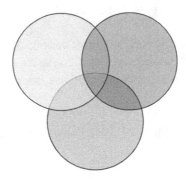

10. **Venn diagrams** (Figure 4.11a and 4.11b) allow students to compare the characteristics of two or three items—what's different, what's the same? Venn diagrams can contain two circles or three circles. Example: Comparing two or three political parties or two or three triangles.

11. **T-charts** (Figure 4.12) allow students to examine two aspects of an issue. These aspects may be pros and cons, advantages or disadvantages, or facts and opinions. Example: The pros and cons of a specific weight management program.

Figure 4.12 T-Chart

T-Chart

+ item	– item
+ item	– item
+ item	– item

There are numerous websites that provide examples and various uses of graphic organizers. Many of these sites furnish templates that allow teachers and students to electronically create and print "personalized" graphic organizers. Several retail stores that sell educational materials have laminated graphic organizers that teachers and students can use and reuse with washable markers.

What Other Types of Visual Representations Do Teachers Use?

In addition to graphic organizers, there are several other types of visual representations. Some of the most commonly used by teachers in their classrooms include:

1. *Photos*: Teachers and students bring in photos from various sources (e.g., magzines, books, personal, online) that represent a current topic or concept.

2. *Technology*: Many commercial curricula offer various areas of technological support. Teachers can also create PowerPoint, Prezi, Camtasia, or other digital presentations incorporating graphics that support and enhance the presentation.

3. *Games*: Vocabulary and other content-related contests with certain rules, which one side or person tries to win. Many of these games replicate common board games or game-style TV shows.

4. *Bulletin boards*: Bulletin boards, walls, windows, whiteboards, and ceilings are all locations where teachers can display items that support the curriculum.

5. *Role playing*: Role playing is a method of instruction in which the students act out real-life situations and discuss and study them.

6. *Models*: Three-dimensional models are excellent instructional tools. They can be used in virtually all content areas, such as anatomical, aerospace, astronomy, biology, chemistry, art, social studies, and mucic.

7. *Sculptures*: Students perform the art of carving or modeling figures associated with the academic content.

8. *Paintings*: Students create original paintings based on the academic content.

9. *Dioramas*: Students create a scene or exhibit, based on the content area, showing a group of lifelike sculptured figures of people, animals, and surrounding objects against a painted or modeled background. Some dioramas are viewed through a window-like opening; others offer a panoramic view.

10. *Costumes*: Students wear outer clothing representative of another time or place, such as is worn on the stage, in historical times, or at masquerades.

11. *Drawings*: Students draw pictures, sketches, plans, or design different elements of the content. Drawings can be done with pencil, pen, chalk, crayon, or charcoal.

12. *Pictographs*: Pictographs are simply pictures that represent a behavior, message, warning, data, information, landmark, word, or feeling. Many road signs and items on maps are pictographs. Numerous digital "apps" and software programs such as Boardmaker can easily be incorporated into instruction or schedules for students with low or no verbal language ability. The advantage of using a pictograph is that it is usually easy to read and understand. What do you suppose these pictographs mean?

Figure 4.13

13. *Kinesthetic*: Physical movement of the legs and arms, representing math angles, body parts, constellations, and words (e.g., balance, diameter), using finger puppets, and role playing are examples of kinesthetic visual representations.

14. *Icons*: In the modern sense, the term icon is generally a recognizable symbol that many people acknowledge as having well-known significance. Computers frequently use icons to guide users. Teachers and students can create icons representing aspects of their area of study. Can you identify these icons?

Figure 4.14

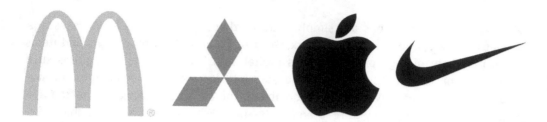

15. *Logos*: Images that are used by companies for brand recognition are important visual representations for a number of reasons. They can be used to develop vocabulary and build confidence as students navigate school and community settings. Some teachers have used logos to familiarize leaerners with the alphabet and support reading instruction.

As you have read in this chapter, there are many effective instructional teaching and learning practices for visual learners. Prentice Hall eTeach (2013) offers a summary of these strategies and tactics:

- Before a lecture, provide students with a general outline of the material to be covered.

- Oral directions with more than two steps should be given on the overhead projector, projection screen, or on the board.

- If you are presenting extensive class notes, hand out a copy of the notes, rather than having students copy volumes from the overhead. In order to ensure that the notes are read and not just stashed with many other unread notes in the notebook, give students an assignment based on the notes or have them make up test items or questions on the notes.

- Use any of the following with each lesson: flip boards, photos, diagrams, or laminated pictures that can be used with group assignments, PowerPoint presentations, charts, maps, movies, filmstrips, time lines, mnemonics.

- Have students construct their own flash cards. Encourage students to illustrate them.

- Provide access to computer programs or CD-ROMs that come with your textbook to provide greater visual exposure and practice.

- Use the computer in the classroom to construct mind maps or webbing of the material. The student can see the material and manipulate it at the same time.

- Use concept maps with key points, boxes, circles, and arrows showing the connections of information. Webbing provides the connections that visual learners must have.

- When doing oral questions and answers in the classroom, allow adequate wait time before calling on students. This is very important for the visual learner, who must retrieve visual images before formulating an answer. If you give them time to determine what you are asking, they will have greater success.

SUMMARY

Most students in a typical classroom are visual learners. Visual learners thrive when teachers use visual repressentations such as charts, graphic organizer maps, mind maps, notes, and flash cards. Graphic organizers are the most common type of visual representations used in classrooms. There are many benefits to students when graphic organizers are used in their classrooms. These benefits include improvements in the following: social skills; process-oriented and strategic learning; questioning ability; reflection and decision making; critical thinking; attitude toward learning; ability to organize thinking; understanding of the different ways to represent and view information; and understanding and retention of content. In addition to graphic organizers, other visual representations include photos, technology, games, role playing, models, pictographs, and various kinesthetics.

With visual learners, they must *see* it to *learn* it!

REVIEW

1. Why should teachers consider using visual representations in their classrooms?

2. What are some visual representations, other than graphic organizers, you would use in your classroom?

3. What are some ways teachers can grade students' graphic organizers?

4. What are some student benefits that result from the use of graphic organizers?

5. At what times during a lesson are graphic organizers used?

6. What are some ways teachers can help students construct their own graphic organizers?

7. Complete the seven templates at the end of this chapter.

REFERENCES

Dye, G. (2000). Graphic organizers to the rescue! *Teaching Exceptional Children*, 32: 1–5.

Fountas, I., & Pinnell, G. (2001). *Guiding readers and writers grades 3–6: Teaching comprehension, genre, and content literacy*. Portsmouth, NH: Heinemann.

Gagnon, J., & Maccini, P. (2000). Best practices for teaching mathematics to secondary students with special needs: Implications from teacher perceptions and a review of the literature. *Focus on Exceptional Children*, 32(5): 1–22.

Gerlic, I., & Jausovec, N. (1999). Multimedia: Differences in cognitive processes observed with EEG. *Educational Technology Research and Development*, 47(3), 5–14.

MindWorks Resources.. www.mindworksresources.com (2013)

Prentice Hall eTeach, Online Education: Something for Everyone, http://www.phschool.com/eteach (2013)

United States Department of Education. (1987). *What works* (2nd ed.). Washington, DC: U.S. Government Printing Office.

The Visual Teaching Alliance, National Office, P.O. Box 2374, Round Rock, TX 78680, www.visualteachingalliance.com (2013)

FIGURE SOURCES

Figure 4.1:
Copyright © 2008 by Lft / Wikimedia Commons / CC BY-SA 3.0
Copyright © 2008 by User:carnavalet / Wikimedia Commons / CC BY-SA 2.0

Figure 4.13:
American Institute of Graphic Arts / Public Domain
U.S. National Park Service / Public Domain
U.S. Department of Transportation / Public Domain
U.S. Department of Transportation / Public Domain
User:Amada44 / Wikimedia Commons / Public Domain
U.S. Department of Transportation / Public Domain

Figure 4.14:
McDonald's / Public Domain
Copyright in the Public Domain
Mitsubishi / Public Domain
Apple / Public Domain
Nike / Public Domain

TEMPLATE 4.1: ALIGNING GRAPHIC ORGANIZERS WITH CONTENT OBJECTIVES

Step 1: Select the grade, course, and unit of your choice.
Step 2: Write a content objective for a lesson within the selected grade, course, and unit.
Step 4: In the space below, create a graphic organizer that provides a complete or partial answer or response to the content objective.

Grade: _____
Course: _____
Unit: _____

Content objective:

Graphic Organizer Example:

TEMPLATE 4.2: PREPARING GRAPHIC ORGANIZERS

Step 1: Select a grade, course, and unit of your choice.
Step 2: Write three different content objectives in the selected grade, course, and unit that would be supported by the corresponding graphic organizer.
Step 3: In the corresponding box create the assigned graphic organizer.

Grade: _____
Course: _____
Unit: _____
Content Objective: _____
Graphic Organizer: Venn Diagram

Content Objective: _____
Graphic Organizer: Sequence of Events

Content Objective: _____
Graphic Organizer: Web

TEMPLATE 4.3: PREPARING GRAPHIC ORGANIZERS

Step 1: Select a grade, course, and unit of your choice.
Step 2: Write three different content objectives in the selected grade, course, and unit that would be supported by the corresponding graphic organizer.
Step 3: In the corresponding box create the assigned graphic organizer.

Grade: _____
Course: _____
Unit: _____
Content Objective: _____
Graphic Organizer: Spider Map

Content Objective: _____
Graphic Organizer: Compare-Contrast Map

Content Objective: _____
Graphic Organizer: Continuum Map

TEMPLATE 4.4: WARM-UP GRAPHIC ORGANIZER

Step 1: Select a grade, course, and unit of your choice.
Step 2: Review Chapter 4, Section: "When Can Graphic Organizers Be Used?"
Step 3: Write a content objective for a lesson within the selected grade, course, and unit.
Step 4: In the space below, create a graphic organizer that would be appropriate for the warm-up phase of the selected unit and content objective.

Grade: _____
Course: _____
Unit: _____
Content objective: _____

Warm-Up Graphic Organizer

TEMPLATE 4.5: DIRECT TEACHING GRAPHIC ORGANIZER

Step 1: Select a grade, course, and unit of your choice.
Step 2: Review Chapter 4, Section: "When Can Graphic Organizers Be Used?"
Step 3: Write a content objective for a lesson within the selected grade, course, and unit.
Step 4: In the space below, create a graphic organizer that would be appropriate for the <u>direct teaching</u> phase of the selected unit and content objective.

Grade: _____
Course: _____
Unit: _____
Content objective: _____

Direct Teaching Graphic Organizer

TEMPLATE 4.6: STUDENT PERFORMANCE GRAPHIC ORGANIZER

Step 1: Select a grade, course, and unit of your choice.
Step 2: Review Chapter 4, Section: "When Can Graphic Organizers Be Used?"
Step 3: Write a content objective for a lesson within the selected grade, course and unit.
Step 4: In the space below, create a graphic organizer that would be appropriate for the student performance phase of the selected unit and content objective.

Grade: _____
Course: _____
Unit: _____
Content objective: _____

Student Performance Graphic Organizer

TEMPLATE 4.7: CLASS REVIEW GRAPHIC ORGANIZER

Step 1: Select a grade, course, and unit of your choice.
Step 2: Review Chapter 4, Section: "When Can Graphic Organizers Be Used?"
Step 3: Write a content objective for a lesson within the selected grade, course, and unit.
Step 4: In the space below, create a graphic organizer that would be appropriate for the class review phase of the selected unit and content objective.

Grade: _____

Course: _____

Unit: _____

Content objective: _____

Class Review Graphic Organizer

Chapter five

STUDENT ENGAGEMENT

While one person hesitates because he feels inferior, the other is busy making mistakes and becoming superior.

—HENRY C. LINK

OBJECTIVES

Readers will be able to:

1. Describe the difference between teaching strategies and learning activities.

2. Describe the positive results of using active teaching strategies and learning activities.

3. Name the language domains to be supported by active teaching strategies and learning activities.

4. Give examples of active teaching strategies and learning activities that are connected to content and language objectives.

5. Describe how to modify active teaching strategies and learning activities in a diverse classroom.

KEY VOCABULARY

Readers will be able to define or describe each term in the context of the chapter information.

| Active Learning | Student Engagement | Teaching Strategies |
| Learning Activities | | |

INTRODUCTION

Creating and implementing effective teaching strategies and learning activities for diverse students in today's classrooms is indeed a challenging task for many teachers. Unfortunately, based on classroom observations by the authors and discussions with other education professionals who observe classrooms, far too many classroom teachers continue to dominate their instruction with lectures, completing worksheets, watching videos, and passive readings. These traditional methods continue to be used, despite the strong evidence that student learning can often be better achieved by using other methods of instruction—namely, student engagement practices (Buehl, 2001; Muth, 1999; O'Malley & Chamot, 1990; Marzano, 2001). Among many educators, the terms active learning and student engagement are used interchangeably. Debate still continues about these terms. Some teachers assert that all "learning" is inherently active, so the method of teaching—whether traditional or nontraditional—is not a factor in defining learning. Others assert that active learning implies that the students are doing more than merely listening, that students are "engaged" by "doing" things that involve skills such as higher-order thinking skills, questioning, analyzing, evaluating, decision making, and problem solving. Thus, this chapter is titled "Student Engagement."

How Do Teachers Lay the Foundation for Student Engagement?

It is easy to observe the lack of student engagement when students are slouched in their chairs and not listening to the teacher or participating in the discussion. Many teachers who constantly see disengaged students put the burden on the student and lament that they could be better teachers and have better results if they had the opportunity to work with a "better" group of students. But classrooms with high levels of student engagement are not simply a result of "student quality" (Jones, 2008).

For teachers to deal with low levels of student performance, they must begin to reflect on the elements that contribute to student engagement. Teachers can have direct control and make changes instantaneously in some areas. For other changes to occur, it will take time for both students and the teacher to develop new skills. Improvements may depend on planning and seeking out new solutions or making changes at the school-wide level (Jones, 2008).

Several common characteristics exist in classrooms where effective student engagement is present. These include:

- Colorful materials

- Student work on walls

- Words, words, words — everywhere

- Movable desks

- Student interactions

- Teacher interactions

- Frequent and multiple groupings

- Student tasks allowing some flexibility (in process and product)

- Demonstration of learning options

- Frequent assessments

- Curriculum connected to students' learning preferences, differences, needs, and interests

- Learning targets posted (content and language)

- Safe

- Academic mistakes are OK

- Encouraging and supportive

- Trying is encouraged

- Learning is expected

- Reading, writing, listening, speaking

- Communication with families

- Challenging expectations

What Are Key Indicators of Engaged Learning?

Engaged learning has been a key element of effective teaching and learning for several years. Eight indicators (and descriptors) designed to help teachers focus their instruction on student engagement were developed by the North Central Regional Educational Laboratory (B. Jones, 1994).

Indicator 1: *Vision of Engaged Learning*

What does engaged learning look like? Successful, engaged learners are responsible for their own learning. These students are self-regulated and able to define their own learning goals and evaluate their own achievement. They are also energized by their learning; their joy of learning leads to a lifelong passion for solving problems, understanding, and taking the next step in their thinking. These learners are strategic in that they know how to learn and are able to transfer knowledge to solve problems creatively. Engaged learning also involves being collaborative—that is, valuing and having the skills to work with others.

Indicator 2: *Tasks for Engaged Learning*

In order to have engaged learning, tasks need to be challenging, authentic, and multidisciplinary. Such tasks are typically complex and involve sustained amounts of time. They are authentic in that they correspond to the tasks in the home and workplaces of today and tomorrow. Collaboration around authentic tasks often takes place with peers and mentors within school, as well as with family members and others in the real world outside of school. These tasks often require integrated instruction that incorporates problem-based learning and curriculum by project.

Indicator 3: *Assessment of Engaged Learning*

Assessment of engaged learning involves presenting students with an authentic task, project, or investigation, and then observing, interviewing, and examining their presentations and artifacts to assess what they actually know and can do. This assessment, often called performance-based assessment, is generative in that it involves students in generating their own performance criteria and playing a key role in the overall design, evaluation, and reporting of their assessment. The best performance-based assessment has a seamless connection to curriculum and instruction so that it is ongoing. Assessment should represent all meaningful aspects of performance and should have equitable standards that apply to all students.

Indicator 4: *Instructional Models and Strategies for Engaged Learning*

The most powerful models of instruction are interactive. Instruction actively engages the learner and extends knowledge. Instruction encourages the learner to construct and produce knowledge in meaningful ways. Students teach others interactively and interact with their teacher and peers. This allows for co-construction of knowledge, which promotes problem-, project-, and goal-based engaged learning. Some common strategies included in engaged learning models of instruction are individual and group summarizing, means of exploring multiple perspectives, techniques for building upon prior knowledge, brainstorming, Socratic dialogue, problem-solving processes, and team teaching.

Indicator 5: *Learning Context of Engaged Learning*

For engaged learning to happen, the classroom must be conceived of as a knowledge-building learning community. Such communities not only develop shared understandings collaboratively, but also create empathetic learning environments that value diversity and multiple perspectives. These communities search for strategies to build on the strengths of all of its members. Truly collaborative classrooms, schools, and communities encourage students to ask hard questions, define problems, lead conversations, set goals, have work-related conversations with family members and other adults in and out of school, and engage in entrepreneurial activities.

Indicator 6: *Grouping for Engaged Learning*

Collaborative work that is learning centered often involves small groups or teams of two or more students within a classroom or across classroom boundaries. Heterogeneous groups (including different sexes, cultures, abilities, ages, and socioeconomic backgrounds) offer a wealth of background knowledge and perspectives to different tasks. Flexible grouping, which allows teachers to reconfigure small groups according to the purposes of instruction and incorporates frequent heterogeneous groups, is one of the most equitable means of grouping and ensuring increased learning opportunities.

Indicator 7: *Teacher Roles for Engaged Learning*

The role of the teacher in the classroom has shifted from the primary role of information-giver to that of facilitator, guide, and learner. As a facilitator, the teacher provides the rich environments and learning experiences needed for collaborative study. The teacher also is required to act as a guide—a role that incorporates mediation, modeling, and coaching. Often the teacher also is a co-learner and coinvestigator with the students.

Indicator 8: *Student Roles for Engaged Learning*

One important student role is that of explorer. Interaction with the physical world and with other people allows students to discover concepts and apply skills. Students are then encouraged to reflect upon their discoveries, which is essential for the student as a cognitive apprentice. Apprenticeship takes place when students observe and apply the thinking processes used by practitioners. Students also become teachers themselves by integrating what they've learned. Hence, they become producers of knowledge, capable of making significant contributions to the world's knowledge.

What Are the Key Elements of Engagement-Based Learning and Teaching (EBLT)?

The EBLT approach (Jones, 2008) encompasses the following six objectives:

1. Cultivate one-on-one relationships. The one-on-one relationship between student and teacher is the critical element that can lead to increased student motivation and higher levels of engagement in academics and school life.

2. Learn new skills and habits. Teachers can learn new skills and habits that help them to develop, polish, and enhance their already natural inclination to motivate and engage students.

3. Incorporate systematic strategies. Teachers can learn systematic strategies that facilitate student engagement. Students can develop behavioral skills and habits that lead to increased academic achievement and greater involvement with school life.

4. Take responsibility for student engagement practices. It is primarily the teacher's responsibility to engage the students, as opposed to the teacher expecting students to come to class naturally and automatically engaged.

5. Promote a school-wide culture of engagement. The best way to promote high levels of student engagement is to develop and maintain a school-wide initiative that is dedicated to creating a culture of student engagement, involving students in school activities, and providing a rigorous and relevant education program for all students.

6. Professional development is an important part of increasing student engagement. Staff development, combined with staff ownership and recognition, is critical to developing and maintaining a culture of effective student engagement.

What Should Teachers Consider When Creating or Selecting Engaging Lessons?

The most important consideration for the teacher is to focus on the targeted content and language objectives. Remembering that a number of the objectives may be modified for some students in the classroom, teachers must create or select lessons that will benefit all students in the classroom. Generally speaking, effective lessons utilize multiple language domains—reading, writing, listening, and speaking—involving multiple presentation practices. Teachers should design their lessons that incorporate and encourage the highest-order thinking skills possible for the targeted students. Whenever possible, teachers should provide ample visual representations (see Chapter 4) of the content. In addition, students should have the opportunity to hear the teacher, video clips, or other students; read the textbook and articles; write (e.g., summaries, note taking, graphic organizers); and talk with partners, in small group discussions, simulations, or in labs about the content. Students should be asked collectively and individually to make decisions and solve problems. In some situations, depending on the learning objective and student proficienies, homogeneous groups (similar ability, language, age, interest) may be more productive than heterogeneous (mixed ability, language, age, interest) groups. In other situations, the opposite may be more productive.

What Are Some Barriers to Using Engaging Lessons?

If traditional classroom practices are deemed less effective, why do some teachers continue to use them? Specific reasons given by teachers as barriers to the use of engaging lessons include limited class time, the need for increased prep time, anxiety, class size, difficulty grading, lack of incentive, insufficient materials or resources, criticism from other teachers, lack of student participation, loss of control of students, students will not learn targeted content for state tests, and lack of necessary skills.

What Do Active and Engaging Teaching Strategies and Learning Activities Mean?

Active and engaging learning activities refers to the level of student participation and involvement in and out of the classroom. Learning important content knowledge and skill is not unlike learning many new skills—be it a physical skill, such as kicking a ball, a mental skill, as in decision making, or a social skill (e.g., communication). Many individuals learn best and become proficient in skills by practicing them rather than merely being a spectator to the skill, such as listening to teachers talk about the skill, reading about the skill, or watching others perform the skill (Hermin & Toth, 2006).

As a quick reminder from Chapter 3, there is a distinction between a teaching strategy and a learning activity. Teaching strategies refer to the structure, system, methods, techniques, procedures, and processes that a teacher uses during instruction. These are strategies the *teacher* employs to assist student learning. Learning activities refer to the teacher-guided instructional tasks or assignments for students. These are *student* activities.

The terms "teaching strategy" and "learning activity" do not exclusively imply active or passive instruction. For example, a teacher may select a lecture teaching strategy, where the students are expected (as their learning activity) to simply listen. Conversely, a teacher may select a problem-based teaching strategy, where the students are expected (as their leaning activity) to discover that they need to learn something in order to solve the problem.

Active and engaging hands-on teaching strategies and learning activities are designed to take students out of their books, sometimes out of their seats, sometimes out of the classroom, sometimes out of their school, and sometimes out of their familiar ways of thinking. Active and engaging hands-on teaching strategies and learning activities are intended to make students active and engaged participants in their own learning (Silberman, 1996; Buehl, 2001).

A sound lesson plan is important for all instruction. However, the lesson plan is crucial when there is an expectation of active and engaged learning. In an active and engaged lesson plan, you will see a lesson that:

1. Represents how real people in the real world need or use this knowledge and/or skill.

2. Provides all students with an opportunity to learn and be successful.

3. Provides students with the opportunity and flexibility to make decisions about how to progress and demonstrate their learning and achievement.

4. Requires several teacher and/or student interactions.

5. Gives students the opportunity to hear and read content and language-learning objectives and allows them to ask clarifying questions about these objectives prior to instruction.

6. Contains objectives that are appropriate to the intellectual, physical, and psychological maturity of the students.

7. Is part of a planned scaffolded teaching strategy involving frequent and multiple student groupings, such as whole class, small groups, partners, and individuals.

8. Contains information and teacher instructions that are clear, concise, relevant, attainable, and appropriate for the students' proficiency.

9. Contains multiple instructional methods with visual learning support.

10. Is linked to students' differences, backgrounds, interests, and prior learning.

11. Is an integral part of the curriculum.

12. Stays on target to address and assess key content understandings and skills.

13. Requires activities that integrate multiple language modalities such as reading, writing, listening, and speaking, as well as various learning preferences.

14. Targets skills and knowledge that are transferable in ways that represent larger learning.

15. Represents high expectations for student learning.

16. Students enjoy and are interested in learning.

17. Students are actively engaged in learning.

18. Assesses students with continuous and multiple methods and tools that contain numerous indicators of learning to reveal what the students know and can do, rather than what the students do not know.

19. Contains multiple materials and resources for diverse learners.

20. Respects the classroom diversity.

21. Ends when learning occurs, not when the "bell" rings.

What Are Some Guidelines for Teachers When Creating Active and Engaging Learning Activities?

Creating an effective active and engaging learning activity is often a challenge for many teachers, especially for individuals in the early stages of their teaching career. A common error results when teachers focus primarily on the "fun" or "active" part of a potential learning activity. As stated previously in this textbook, the primary focus for the teacher (and students) should be the targeted learning objective(s). What often happens when teachers tend to focus on the "fun" or "active" side is the learning objective gets lost. For example, the authors have observed countless situations where teachers have created an active lesson where the "active" part was so energetic and lively that it overshadowed the actual learning that it was intended to achieve.

Teachers should consider several questions when selecting or developing active learning activities in diverse-ability classrooms (adapted from Wandberg & Rohwer, 2010):

1. What is the grade level?

2. What are the students' ability levels (for example, 21 students are on level, two students are above level, five students are Level 3 ELL students, and two students are below level).

3. What is the content area, the unit, and the topic?

4. What is the title of the student activity?

5. Using clear, concise, specific, relevant, attainable, and measurable terms, what are the lesson's content objectives (typically taken from national, state, or local standards or guidelines)?

6. Using clear, concise, specific, relevant, attainable, and measurable terms, what are the lesson's language objectives (focusing on reading, writing, listening, and speaking)?

7. Provide an overview description of the active learning lesson. This description should provide enough detail so that a substitute teacher could successfully implement the instruction.

8. How much classroom time will the students have to complete the lesson? This may be indicated in minutes, such as 35 minutes, or in classes (e.g., four class periods).

9. What materials are needed? Having the correct and sufficient number of instructional materials is vital to the lesson's success. Materials may include such items as computer needs (i.e., screen, adapters, wires, extension cords), printed materials, such as articles or worksheets, production needs, including tape, scissors, magazines, markers, chart paper, and audio-visual equipment (i.e., DVD, VCR, TV).

10. How will the students be grouped or organized? Will students work independently or in groups? What will be the size of each group of students? Will students be grouped randomly, by language ability, or some other way? Chapter 6, Grouping and Cooperative Learning, will provide detailed information on student grouping options.

11. What is the suggested furniture arrangement for this lesson? Is there a need to move the students' desks into another arrangement, such as small group circles, rows, teams, or perimeter?

12. What specific directions will be given to the students before the lesson begins? How will these be given? Giving clear student directions is often a more difficult process than teachers anticipate. Here are some suggestions for giving clear student directions:

- Have the attention of the class while directions are being given.

- Provide directions in both verbal and written form.

- Make sure the students know what they are expected to learn.

- Give the directions in sequential order.

- Use visuals to help students follow a sequence of steps.

- Refrain from overdirecting.

- Be clear about the consequences of good work.

- Ask selected students to repeat the directions.

- Allow time for students to ask questions about the directions.

- Do not allow students to start the activity until the process of giving directions is completed.

13. What specific directions will be given to the students after the lesson begins? How will these be given (both written and orally are best)? How will the teacher stop the student activity to provide additional student information and/or directions?

14. What product is expected from the students at the completion of the lesson? Students should have a clear understanding of what demonstration of learning is expected at the end of the activity. Will it be a completed worksheet, role play, summary, problem solved, decision made, poster, brochure, PowerPoint, or other digital presentation, game, survey, or report?

15. What are the students' and the lesson's expectations, such as noise level, use of equipment and materials, time limit, sharing of responsibilities, and the return of materials? In addition to orally explaining, posting the students' responsibilities often helps the students to have a clear understanding of their expectations.

16. What will be the teacher's role in this lesson? The teacher should have a clear understanding what instructional role—whether it be assessing, evaluating, facilitating, coaching, or encouraging—he or she will have while the students are actively engaged in their learning activity.

17. What additional information is needed to make this lesson successful? Some active teaching strategies and learning activities have unique components that require specialized equipment, time, or materials. For example, as compared to an in-class lesson, there are typically some unique instructional issues to consider when a teacher takes his or her health education high school students to a neighboring elementary school to conduct a cross-age teaching lesson.

18. How will student assessment information be obtained? Gathering information to determine the degree of student learning, achievement, and success is a complex task. A language-diverse classroom exaggerates this complexity. Assessments, the gathering of information, can be informal or formal. Examples of informal assessments would include quick voting, thumbs up/thumbs down, raising hands, and random classroom and/or student observations. See Chapter 8, Assessment and Grading, for more detailed information.

What Are Examples of Active Teaching Strategies and Learning Activities?

There are many active teaching strategies and learning activities that can be effectively used in a diverse classroom. This chapter section names, describes, and gives examples of several common active teaching strategies and learning activities that can support many content and language-learning objectives. The activities are listed in alphabetical order. Each activity includes a brief description and example. When necessary, teachers are encouraged to adjust and modify these activities to better meet specific student needs and their targeted student-learning objectives (Bergs, adapted with permission, 2005).

Assignments with Choice strategies allow students to decide how they will demonstrate that they have learned the required information and/or skill. Some students may choose to demonstrate their learning by writing, others by speaking, others by drawing or illustrating, and others by building. For example, there may be multiple ways that a student could demonstrate his or her knowledge of the solar system.

A–Z Taxonomy is a language strategy. In small groups, students list the 26 letters A through Z vertically on a piece of paper. Then, based on the specific content, students are asked to think of terms associated with that content that start with each of the letters. For example, in the content area of math, students might list (A) axis, (B) binomial, (C) coefficient, (D) dependent, (E) exponent, and so on. This activity can be used as both a pre- and post-instructional technique.

Best Choice Debate is a strategy that asks pairs of students to first prepare either a pro or con position on a controversial issue, such as abortion. A pro pair and a con pair then join to explain their positions to each other and then to seek agreement on the group's best overall recommendation. The benefit of this type of strategy is that it provides speaking and listening opportunities, as well as practice in the skill of negotiation and compromise.

Brainstorming is a simple strategy designed to draw out numerous, creative, original, imaginative, innovative, resourceful, and inventive ideas. These may be responses to content-related, open-ended questions, issues, or problems. Teachers should encourage all students to participate. In language-diverse classrooms, some students may feel more comfortable responding as part of a small team of students. Because the intent of brainstorming is to solicit lots of ideas, no students should be criticized for their idea(s). Sometimes it helps to set an appropriate target number of ideas—say, eight—when asking, for example, what lifestyle habits can cause premature death. Another strategy to use when students are having difficulty generating ideas is to reverse the statement (e.g., what things might cause premature death?).

Building Teamwork is a strategy that asks small groups of students to prepare a group résumé consisting of items such as hobbies, talents, travel, awards, favorite classes, schools attended, siblings, and any other information a student wishes to share. This strategy is designed to show the diversity of experiences and abilities in the class. In addition to the general categories listed above, content-related questions focusing on items such as favorite foods, sports, subjects, past injuries, and other related topics could be included.

Carousel Questions is a strategy where the teacher writes several questions about a content topic on large sheets of paper posted around the room. In small groups, students rotate (e.g., every five minutes) from one set of questions to the next. Each group of students has a different colored marker. At each station, the team adds ideas—answers—responses to the paper that have not been previously listed. Share all responses when the activity concludes. For example, what are the benefits of the geographic areas that contain rain forests?

Case Studies use real-life stories that describe what happened to a community, family, school, or individual to prompt students to apply their content knowledge and skill to authentic, real-world attitudes, behaviors, and consequences.

Character Maps are ideal for some content-related information and concepts. Students, individually or with a partner, draw a stick figure or snowman-shaped body on their paper.

Students are asked to label or generate information related to the body. For example, draw and label the traits of the main characters in the story.

Cooperative Learning is a strategy that involves small groups of students working together to complete a project or task. Teachers using this instructional strategy often assign specific roles, duties, and tasks to specific group members. The grouping configuration may be random, voluntary, or teacher assigned. Grouping configurations should change frequently throughout the term. Teachers should appropriately group students based on the group task and student abilities. See Chapter 6 for additional information and examples.

Critical Explanation asks students to think about factors or reasons that might explain the cause of some content-related issue or problem. The key word is *might*. Do not use a word (such as *why*) that suggests there are right or wrong answers or that there is just one answer. Question triggers could include the following: What might explain ...? Can you think of reasons ...? For example, what might explain the rise in childhood obesity?

Discussion Web is a teaching and learning technique where students consider a content-related problem (e.g., rank choice voting) in a small group and then regroup so each student can share his or her group's work with students who were in different task groups. After all groups have completed their work, students decide who is A and who is B. Teachers then ask the As to remain seated and the Bs to stand and find a new A to be your partner. A and B share information.

Field Studies provide students with an opportunity to learn about and study issues in their community. Areas of study may include various community and governmental products and services.

Forced Debate asks all students who agree with a content-related issue (e.g., global warming) to sit or stand on one side of the room and all opposed on the other side. Often, hanging a sign on each side of the room helps to keep the issue clarified. After students have selected their position, switch the signs and force them to argue for the issue with which they disagree. This strategy will force the groups to consider an opposing viewpoint. Avoid predictability by varying the times when you switch, or do not switch, the signs.

Games can often be used to reinforce content-related knowledge. Student-generated games can be both fun to create and play. Games can follow any common board or TV format. Games can involve matching, mysteries, group or individual competitions, and puzzles or follow the format of games such as Pictionary, Jeopardy!, Wheel of Fortune, Family Feud, Clue, and Scrabble.

Graphic Organizers are visual representations of important facts, concepts, and vocabulary and how they are linked (or not linked) together. Graphic organizers can be effectively used as a focusing, primary, review, or assessment activity. Teach students how to create and construct their own graphic organizers. Ask students to identify the main words, ideas, sections, or content and determine relationships between and among them; then determine the style format of the graphic organizer that is most appropriate for the material and purpose. Students should use icons and pictures, as well as words in their graphic organizer, and when possible, students should use a variety of colors to represent different aspects of their graphic organizers. See Chapter 4 for more detailed information and examples.

Group Summarizing is a strategy that asks students, in small groups, to summarize a content-related reading or observation (e.g., magazine article, text section, and/or video).

Younger students may need predetermined summarizing categories, such as major topics, concepts, facts, and time lines. Summaries may be described in text or graphic format.

Group Work allows every student the chance to speak, to share ideas and information, and to develop the skill of working with others. Cooperative work groups require all students to work together to complete a given task. Typical cooperative group tasks include articles to read, questions to answer and discuss, information to share, subjects to teach to other groups, the creation of projects, problem solving, and decision making. Assigning and rotating various student roles are often helpful with this activity. See Chapter 6 for more detailed information.

Guided Reciprocal Peer Questioning is a strategy where teachers provide students with several sentence starters. Each student selects one or two sentence starters and creates a complete question based on the material covered in class. The students do not actually have to know the answer to the question they are creating. Group students discuss the questions each student has created. The purpose is to generate discussion. Sentence starters may include what is …, where is …, what can you say about …, give reasons for …, what are the parts of …, what is another way …, what is your opinion of …, how can you use …, what is the main idea of …, or why do you think …, and so forth.

"I Say" Review is a strategy that asks pairs of students to share what they have to say about a content-related topic (such as water pollution) rather than what is the correct answer to a question. This can be used as a pre- or post-strategy. This strategy can also be used early in the term to create a more relaxed attitude toward speaking and sharing.

Inside-Outside Circle is a technique to encourage speaking about and listening to a topic. Depending on the size of the class, one, two, or three circles can be used. Have five to ten students stand in a circle facing outward. Match with five to ten students in an outside circle, facing a partner on the inside circle. First, for 30 seconds, outside-circle students tell their partners some content-related information or their opinion (e.g., ways to view constellations). Next, for ten seconds, the inside group summarizes the information received. Then, the outside circle moves one (or two) students around the inside circle and repeats. (Hint: Vary which circle moves and which circle gives information.)

KWL is a common strategy that can be productive in many classrooms. The teachers or students make a three-column graphic with the labels K (What I Know), W (What I Want to Find Out), and L (What I Learned). Students brainstorm what they know about a particular content-related topic (e.g., the U.S. Constitution); next, individually, with partners, or in small groups, they generate questions about what they still want to know; and finally, they read and gather information that answers their questions.

Logical Analogies is a strategy where students try to find connections or analogies between a content-related fact or concept and a non–content-related fact or concept using this format: How is _____ like _____? For example, how is your nervous system like a telephone system? Ask students to generate the analogy statements. Here are some possible ending ideas: How is _____ like running for political office, running a marathon, having your first date, fighting a disease, going on a diet, building a house, going fishing, or learning a new language?

Minute Papers provide students with the opportunity to summarize their content-related knowledge and to ask unanswered questions. Give students a minute or two in the middle or at the end of class to answer questions (in writing), such as the following: What was the most important thing you learned today? What can you say about …? What is your opinion of ...? What important question remains unanswered? Use student answers to help plan upcoming lessons.

Music Memory is a strategy that uses familiar ballads and songs. Commercials often use familiar music and songs to promote their products. Many children remember the ABCs song. Ask students to create a song, ballad, or jingle that will help them remember important information, such as content-related facts, dates, formulas, rules, names, vocabulary pronunciations, or sequences (e.g., steps in solving a math problem).

Numbered Students is a small group (three to five students) activity where each student in the group is given a number (1, 2, 3, 4, or 5). The teacher asks a question and randomly chooses a number. The student with that number answers the question for his or her group. The teacher should select a higher-order thinking question, such as, "What is the healthiest food you ate yesterday, and how do you know?"

One-Minute Club is a review strategy designed to support the language domain of speaking. Often at the beginning of the term, the one-minute club should be reduced and referred to as the "15-Second Club." The time should then be gradually increased throughout the term. Teacher- and/or student-generated content-related words or questions are placed in a hat or something similar. Ask for student volunteers, or select students to draw one out and talk about it for one minute (or 15 seconds). A pause of three seconds or more, or the use of "um" or "ah" for three seconds results in disqualification. Choose easier words or questions at the beginning of the term to instill confidence, especially for the ELL students. For example, what is meant by the term "reptile," and give two examples.

Outcome Sentences are often used following videos or guest speakers. Ask students to complete a couple of questions, such as I learned ..., I was surprised ..., I'm feeling ..., or I would like to learn more about ...

Paired Discussions are designed as a quick strategy in which students quickly discuss with their partner information that summarizes the class content recently presented. The activity prompt can be general or specific, depending on the desired outcome or content.

Pass the Q & A is a good strategy for diverse students. To emphasize important content-related information, the teacher suddenly announces a question and the answer. Then, all students pass the question and answer along, with one student asking the question, the next answering it. Sample question: What do the letters BMI stand for? Answer: Body Mass Index.

Peer or Cross-Age Tutoring can be done individually or in pairs. Students provide assistance to others in helping them to better understand content-related concepts. As the name implies, students assist other students who are about the same age, younger students, older students, or students with other educational needs, such as ELLs. Student tutors should try to use graphic organizers whenever possible as a way to visually represent the content-related concepts.

Persistence Celebrations allow the students to relax for a few minutes to celebrate the completion of a successful assignment, challenge, or task. The celebration could involve a simple stand, walk around the room, stretch, class cheer, listening/singing along to a popular song, shaking hands, giving high fives, or letting the class determine the unique way they want to celebrate their achievements.

Picture Making is similar to a graphic organizer. The teacher selects a content-related concept or information that could be visually illustrated. Small groups of students create a visual illustration of the information or concept on the board or on paper. When completed, groups share and discuss their illustration with other groups or the entire class. For example, the concept could be "children inherit genetic traits from their parents."

Practice Test Question is a strategy where the teacher gives the students a sample exam question for practice and then asks several students at random to report their answers to the class. Giving the students a chance to practice the types of questions they might see on your test will give them more confidence when they have to work them alone.

Pre-Reading Predictions is a strategy that allows the students, individually or in small groups, to make predictions about an upcoming reading assignment. For instance, a teacher may select and share a few unfamiliar words from the reading and ask students to predict what the reading is about. Terms such as "pathogen," "incubation," "prognosis," "host," and "immune" might be selected.

Problem-Based Learning is a strategy where a problem drives the learning. Students are presented with a problem prior to learning the problem-associated knowledge or skill. Students must then decide on and find the information they need to solve the problem. Sample problem: What are the best ways to reduce water pollution?

Reaction Response is a quick strategy where the teacher, after presenting a controversial topic, asks students to write or orally respond to a question, such as the following: What information do you question? What information is new? Students can complete this individually or in small groups. Ask for volunteers to share their responses.

Role Playing is a common strategy where the teacher asks several students to take on the roles of participants in the content-related situations being studied. This strategy can be used to demonstrate problem-solving and decision-making skills. Depending on the topic, the role play can be spontaneous, or students might need some time to prepare. In more elaborate role play, students may require a few days to research and prepare for their roles. It is often important to remind students of the specific purpose of this activity.

Rotation Questioning is a technique where the last student speaking calls on the next student to be the speaker. For example, student A selects and asks student B a question related to the content-related topic (e.g., the solar system). When student B completes his or her answer, he or she calls on student C to ask a question. Student C selects and asks student D a question, and so on.

Roundtable Writing is a small-group writing and speaking idea-seeking strategy in which students take turns writing on a single sheet of paper. Each student says their idea aloud as they write it on the paper, then the student passes the paper to the next student, and so on. Sample question: How can residential recycling be improved?

Sign Language is a strategy that often helps ELL students. Students are asked to generate hand or body signs for key content-related vocabulary. Every time you or your students say the word, use the sign as well. Start with common terms such as *river, stream, lake, ocean, mountain,* and *valley*. For instance, every time the teacher (or student) mentions the word *river*, the teacher and students make a wave motion with their hands.

Silence, Please involves a teacher giving directions to his or her students without speaking. These directions can be for an upcoming project, task, or assignment. As an option, ask students to respond to a question the same way—no speaking, actions only!

Speak or Pass is a quick strategy where students are presented with a content-related question, such as, name a former president of the United States. Ask each student, in turn, in a row or class section, to answer the question. Each student can answer the question or say, "I pass."

Question Starters, Prompts, and Triggers help students frame and provide answers to questions that go beyond yes/no responses. Question starters, prompts, and triggers can be low-level questions, such as define, label, name, tell, show, select, or underline. These question starters, prompts, and triggers can also be higher level, such as evaluate, design, defend, summarize, or predict.

Stay or Stray is a small-group strategy where four to six small groups of students read, discuss, and write down information related to a different, but specific, component of a content-related issue or topic, such as AIDS. One group might read, discuss, and write the cause of AIDS; another group, AIDS transmission; another, signs and/or symptoms; and another, treatment. When groups are finished, one person (e.g., the student wearing the most red or the student who has a May birthday, for instance) is randomly selected to "stay." The rest of the group "strays" to the next group. The remaining individual informs the new group about the topic. After a few minutes, the teacher announces which students from the new groups will stay (e.g., a student who has the letter K in his or her name) and which students will stray. As you can see, each student must pay attention to the person speaking because he or she may be the next to stay and have to share the information with the new group.

Student Self-Evaluation is a strategy where the students write a brief evaluation of their assignments, projects, and/or learning. Depending on the activity to be evaluated, it may be helpful to use sentence triggers focusing on the activity, such as problems encountered, reasons, organization or learning process, opinions, or suggesting another way.

Student-Developed Case Studies allow for students, individually or in small groups, to develop a case study of a real or fictional situation that presents an issue or problem. Case studies can then be shared with other students or groups for reactions or solutions.

Test Questions allow students, individually or in small groups, to write test questions about the content-related topics covered in class. To encourage a wide range of thinking, students should write several different question formats, such as multiple choice, true or false, essay, completion, or short answer. When completed, students or small groups exchange tests, or groups can present their questions to the entire class. Teachers can collect the questions and use the best ones on the real test.

Think-Alouds help students in a thinking process. For example, the teacher, in reading or describing a content-related problem, illustrates the problem-solving thinking processes out loud (verbally) for all students to hear. This strategy can be especially helpful with new vocabulary terms or sequential processes. A teacher describing the formula for determining target heart range should say the thinking steps out loud, such as "First, I want to determine maximum heart rate; I will write down my base number 220 (male) or 224 (female); next, I will write down my age; I will then subtract my age from my base number ..." and so on.

Think-Pair-Share is a simple strategy you can use with many topics and in many classroom situations. Give students time to think about a topic (e.g., why do some doctors smoke?) for a few minutes, then turn to their neighbor for a short discussion, and then share the results with the rest of the class.

Thirty-Second Sound Bite for Radio or TV is an activity where, individually or in small groups, students prepare a 30-second announcement designed to get the attention of students and/or listeners about a content-related issue, such as bullying.

Three-Minute Pause strategies are often used when the teacher is presenting some detailed or complex content. After a period of teacher presentation time (e.g., ten minutes), have students pair with a partner and answer a sentence trigger, such as "Discuss with your partner the main ideas of the presentation." For example, discuss with your partner the functions of the vitamins described in the presentation, or how many heart disease risk factors can you list. After three minutes, return to presenting more health content.

Truth Statements is a strategy often used at the beginning of a new unit or topic. Ask individuals or small groups of students to generate three facts they already know about a specific topic (e.g., astronomy, geology, or meteorology). Share the ideas and facts.

Value Continua provide students with an opportunity to physically line up according to how strongly they agree or disagree with a controversial issue. To help students get accustomed to this strategy, it is often a good idea to first select a low-emotion issue, such as "I love roller skating." Ask for student volunteers to share their viewpoints and for the other students to listen to the differing viewpoints. After a while, the teacher can move to more emotionally intense topics, such as gun registration, euthanasia, or drug testing.

Who Am I? is a strategy to help students learn content. Students should be divided into two or more teams. Put several content-related names or terms on a piece of paper. Examples include the following:

I am _____. Supply a content-related person, such as William Shakespeare.

I am _____. Supply a content-related event, such as first human heart transplant.

I am _____. Supply a content-related skill, such as CPR.

I am _____. Supply a content-related quotation, such as "Some are born great, some achieve greatness, and some have greatness thrust upon them."

I am _____. Supply a content-related formula, such as determining the area of a triangle.

I am _____. Supply a content-related risk factor, such as texting while driving.

I am _____. Supply a content-related condition, such as tuberculosis.

I am _____. Supply a nutrient such as Vitamin C.

I am _____. Supply a content-related specialist, such as a geologist.

Select students to randomly choose a piece of paper. Each team, in order, asks the student a yes-or-no question. The team that correctly identifies the term wins that round of the activity. Repeat with other students. As a competition option, keep track of team points.

Word Sorting often helps students—especially language learners—recognize relation-ships between and among content-related terms. Students are given several terms and a few categories from a unit or topic. Their task, individually or in small groups, is to group and place the terms in the categories. As an option, students are given only the terms and then asked to group the terms in ways that make sense to them, and finally to generate a category name for each group. For example, drug-related terms, fitness-related terms, and body-system terms work well for this type of activity.

Write a Question is a strategy used following a presentation by the teacher or student. Instead of asking "Are there any questions?" ask each student to write down two questions. The two questions may be questions the students still have about the topic, or they may be two test questions on the topic. Ask students to share questions with a partner, a small group, or the entire class.

There are many teaching strategies and learning activities that can be employed to assist student learning. Not all strategies and activities are equally effective. Some will be more successful with some students and less successful with others. Some will be more effective than others in providing content information. Some will support the development of skills better than others. Some will offer more language support than others. And finally, some will be more conducive to providing assessment information. By learning and practicing the various teaching strategies and learning activities, teachers will soon realize which are most productive in given situations.

The primary task of the teacher is to design engaging tasks and activities for students that call upon them to learn what the school has determined they should learn, and then leading students to success in the completion of these tasks. Teachers are, therefore, designers and leaders, and the role of teacher must be redefined to reflect this view. To redefine the role of teacher, it will also be necessary to redesign every other role.

While it may sometimes be efficient to have students listen to a short lecture, view video material, or read a textbook, doing these types of isolating, sedentary activities on a regular basis becomes mind numbing rather than mind engaging. There are strategies that naturally contribute to a much higher level of student engagement. For example, cooperative learning strategies, in which students are organized into structured discussion groups and play specific roles in analyzing problems and seeking solutions, are more engaging than listening to a lecture. Moreover, varying instructional strategies adds interest and increases engagement. However, if done continually, even the most exciting activities lose their appeal.

SUMMARY

Creating and implementing effective teaching strategies and learning activities for diverse students in general education classrooms is indeed a challenging task for many teachers. When creating or selecting active and engaging student lessons, the most important consideration for the teacher is to focus on the targeted content and language objectives. Effective active and engaging student lessons utilize all of the multiple language domains—reading, writing, listening, and speaking. Teachers should design their lessons so that they incorporate and encourage the highest-order thinking skills possible for the targeted students.

REVIEW

1. Provide a brief description of an active and engaging learning activity that focuses on the language modality of reading.

2. Provide a brief description of an active and engaging learning activity that focuses on the language modality of writing.

3. Provide a brief description of an active and engaging learning activity that focuses on the language modality of listening.

4. Provide a brief description of an active and engaging learning activity that focuses on the language modality of speaking.

5. Name five characteristics that exist in classrooms where effective student engagement is present.

6. Name five important items you would see in an active and engaged lesson.

7. Complete the four templates at the end of this chapter.

REFERENCES

Bergs, M. *Working with English language learners*. (2005). Mankato, MN: Limited Liability Corporation.

Buehl, D. (2001). *Classroom strategies for interactive learning* (2nd ed.). Newark, DE: International Reading Association.

Hermin, M., & Toth, M. (2006). *Inspiring active learning: A complete handbook for teachers*. Alexandria, VA: Association for Supervision and Curriculum Development (ASCD).

Jones, B., Valdez, G., Nowakowski, J., & Rasmussen, C. (1994). *Designing learning and technology for educational reform*. Oakbrook, IL: North Central Regional Educational Laboratory.

Jones, R. (2008). *Strengthening Student Engagement*, International Center for Leadership in Education, www.leadered.com/pdf/strengthen%20student%20engagement%20white%20paper.pdf

Marzano, R., Pickering, D., & Pollock, J. (2001). Classroom instruction that works: Research-based strategies for increasing student achievement. Alexandria, VA: ASCD.

Muth, K. D., & Alvermann, D. E. (1999). *Teaching and learning in the middle grades*. Needham Heights, MA: Allyn & Bacon.

O'Malley, J. J., & Chamot, A. U. (1990). *Learning strategies in second language acquisition*. Cambridge, UK: Cambridge University Press.

Silberman, M. (1996). *Active learning: 101 strategies to teach any subject*. Needham Heights, MA: Allyn & Bacon.

Wandberg, R., and Rohwer, J. (2010). *Teaching health education in language diverse classrooms*. Sudbury, MA: Jones and Bartlett Publishers.

TEMPLATE 5.1: ALIGNING ACTIVE LEARNING WITH LANGUAGE MODALITIES

Step 1: Select a grade, course, unit, and language objective of your choice
Step 2: Provide a brief description of an engaging learning activity that supports your selected grade, course, and unit that focuses on the language modality of <u>writing</u>.

Grade: _____
Course: _____
Unit: _____

Language Objective:

Writing

TEMPLATE 5.2: ALIGNING ACTIVE LEARNING WITH LANGUAGE MODALITIES

Step 1: Select a grade, course, unit, and language objective of your choice
Step 2: Provide a brief description of an engaging learning activity that supports your selected grade, course, and unit that focuses on the language modality of <u>speaking</u>.

Grade: _____
Course: _____
Unit: _____

Language Objective:

Speaking

TEMPLATE 5.3: ALIGNING ACTIVE LEARNING WITH LANGUAGE MODALITIES

Step 1: Select a grade, course, unit, and language objective of your choice
Step 2: Provide a brief description of an engaging learning activity that supports your selected grade, course, and unit that focuses on the language modality of <u>listening</u>.

Grade: _____
Course: _____
Unit: _____

Language Objective:

Listening

TEMPLATE 5.4: ALIGNING ACTIVE LEARNING WITH LANGUAGE MODALITIES

Step 1: Select a grade, course, unit, and language objective of your choice
Step 2: Provide a brief description of an engaging learning activity that supports your selected grade, course, and unit that focuses on the language modality of <u>reading</u>.

Grade: _____
Course: _____
Unit: _____

Language Objective:

Reading

Chapter six

GROUPING AND COOPERATIVE LEARNING

Common sense and personal experiences suggest that one size rarely fits all. A single instructional response to a group of diverse learners often means that the teaching technique will help some while it ignores others. Furthermore, the exclusive use of the single instructional technique over time will magnify that flaw.

—MICHAEL FORD, 1995

OBJECTIVES

Readers will be able to:

1. Identify grouping models that facilitate learning.

2. Create learning groups based on the purpose of the instruction.

3. Discuss how various models of co-teaching impact grouping practices.

KEY VOCABULARY

Readers will be able to define or describe each term in the context of the chapter information:

Class-Wide Peer Tutoring (CWPT)	Heterogeneous Group	Reciprocal Teaching
Connected Literature Circles	Homogeneous Group	Targeted Instruction
Cooperative Learning	Intensive Instruction	Universal Instruction
Flexible Grouping	Jigsaw Groups	

INTRODUCTION

Third-grade teacher Sam looked at his seating chart and then around at his room. He was told that he would be receiving a new student in his already full classroom. With 29 little bodies (17 boys and 12 girls) in the room, in addition to the bookshelf of leveled readers, two computers, a file cabinet, and a few other odds and ends, he wondered exactly how to not only arrange the room, but how to group students in meaningful ways. Sam almost always used the desk buddies system (four students sitting together in a quad) as groups because it seemed to cause less disruption.

Three of the boys and one little girl were *very* active. Sam had them scattered around the room, but wondered if he should put them in a quad of their own. There was a cluster of five girls who were always tattling on each other; some days they liked each other, some days they didn't. There was a little boyfriend-girlfriend situation that he watched carefully. One of Sam's students was recently diagnosed with childhood rheumatoid arthritis and may need to have braces or a wheelchair. Another student wore hearing aids, and Sam wore a transmitter. The language learners in the class, the students on IEPs and others at risk—as well as the students who were starting to exhibit real academic and creative talents—made Sam think hard and long about the classroom setup and his grouping practices. What should he do?

"And, oh by the way," his principal reminded him as he handed over paperwork on the new student, "Sam, you are a candidate for a co-teaching arrangement." What would that mean?

Incorporating a variety of grouping models and cooperative learning during a day provides opportunities for diverse students to be engaged in classroom instruction. Groups can be used across content areas, ability, and age levels. The purpose of a group will determine the model selected. Grouping students can facilitate instruction and learning, whether one or more teachers are in a classroom. Well-designed groups and cooperative learning opportunities require advance planning. Most recently, flexible grouping practices have been identified with differentiation. Flexible grouping is not static (Radencich & McKay, 1995), but rather, it acknowledges that all grouping patterns have value because they offer different experiences with different outcomes.

What Is the Purpose of Using Different Grouping Models to Create an Instructional Environment?

Teachers use groups for different reasons. Grouping students supports differentiation. Class size can be intimidating to some students and inhibit participation. Children who have difficulty processing information, those who are introverted as a result of an emotional impairment, speech, or language difference, or students who attend to everything around them in the room may benefit from a variety of grouping situations. According to Kaufman and Wandberg (2010), "Group work allows every student the chance to speak, share ideas and information, and develop the skill of working with others" (p. 91).

Three fundamental reasons exist for grouping students:

Student engagement: Participation in discussions and hands-on learning experience is enhanced through group work. If the purpose of grouping students is to increase opportunities for them to interact with content and show what they know in a less threatening way, well-designed small groups can accomplish that purpose. Smaller student groups established within a classroom have a way of promoting discussion and explanations that use more age-appropriate or child-friendly vocabulary as work is completed. Within the instructional environment as a whole, as the level of trust and emotional safety increases, so will the student's willingness to speak up and share.

Social interaction: For some students with disabilities, it is important to create groups that build social interaction. Aside from being in school, there may be few opportunities to make friends or develop age-level, socially appropriate skills. General education classrooms provide settings where real-time instruction and modeling of behaviors can be facilitated in small groups. The benefits also extend to general education students. Interaction between students with disabilities and their peers without disabilities opens doors to understanding and reinforces positive social skills for all students. In an era when concerns about bullying prevail inside and outside of school, both face to face and electronically, using groups to build the social skills of all students is crucial. Author Robert Perske and illustrator Martha Perske share stories of social groupings in the book *Circle of Friends*, demonstrating how people with disabilities and their friends enrich the lives of one another (Abingdon Press, 1988).

Collaborative work: Projects lend themselves nicely to collaborative group work. Strengths of different students can be utilized to accomplish tasks within the project. For example, if a student with a cognitive impairment is assigned to work with peers, distributing and collecting materials associated with the project may be the responsibility of one student. Another may be tasked with the use of the computer or equipment needed to conduct the research. A third student may be responsible for any illustrations needed to document the steps. Each of the roles and duties would be clearly identified and discussed prior to the start of the project. Collaborative work requires skills in communication, decision making, and problem solving. Everyone benefits from these.

Multiple grouping configurations exist within each of the three main purposes. Reasons for using different groups may change as the classroom dynamics change during the year or as the content and instructional needs differ. Thinking through the grouping options and considering ways to troubleshoot before something becomes a problem is a practice used by effective teachers. Some suggestions are given in Table 6.1. What are other practices that will assist in troubleshooting?

Table 6.1 Grouping Purposes and Troubleshooting

PURPOSES	IDEAS FOR USING THIS:	TROUBLESHOOTING:
Student Engagement	• Class management • Content instruction • Assessment	• Set time limits • Clear guidelines • Change groups
Social Interaction	• Friendly competition • Team building	• Ensure all students are involved
Collaborative Work	• Projects	• Identify roles of group members

How Will I Know What Types of Groups to Use?

Teachers may determine there are times when students should be grouped with those more like them in ability, and other times when groups of very diverse students are necessary to achieve the designated tasks and purposes. What is the recommended number of students per group? It is recommended that three to five students in a group work well. Smaller groups accomplish the work more efficiently and tend to be more accountable. The roles and responsibilities can readily be assigned and are more transparent. Some groups may consist of six to ten participants (such as content groups) and will depend on the purpose of the group, physical facilities, or presence of a co-teacher.

What are Options for Grouping Students?

There are many options to implement flexible grouping in a classroom. The choice of a group size depends on the instructional purpose as well as the needs of the students in the class.

Pairs

Paired instruction may mean a one-on-one opportunity for the teacher to work with a student on direct, intensive instruction and immediate feedback. Or it may mean a quick think-pair-share to stimulate brain energy. Paired reading provides a built-in partner during language arts. Study buddies offer students the opportunity to ask questions and study content together for an upcoming test.

Reciprocal Teaching

This is a paired or small-group practice between teachers and students. Palincsar (1986) described reciprocal teaching as an instructional practice where a portion of a text is studied as teacher and student(s) engage in dialogue. Four procedures are used to structure the discussion. Each procedure assists students in constructing meaning from text and ensures they understand what is read. The four procedures are:

1. Summarizing: Students must identify and integrate the most important information in the text. A teacher may ask a student to summarize across sentences, across paragraphs, or across the passage as a whole. The level of difficulty increases as the amount of text to summarize increases.

2. Question generating: To generate questions, students identify significant and substantial information from the text. The student provides both the questions and the answers. Teachers may ask students to focus on detailed information or to infer new information from the text.

3. Clarifying: In this procedure, students become aware of the many reasons why text can be difficult to understand and are taught how to overcome these barriers. For instance, they note new vocabulary, reference words that may be confusing (e.g., using "these" "those" or other words to "refer" to a previously named noun) and unfamiliar or difficult concepts. Methods to assist students in building independence might include using context clues, rereading the segment, or asking for help.

4. Predicting: To successfully predict what the author will discuss next in the text, students must be cognizant of the relevant background knowledge that they already possess regarding the topic. The predicting strategy also makes use of text structure, as students learn that headings, subheadings, and questions embedded in the text are useful means of anticipating what might occur next.

Ability Groups

In some classrooms, teachers match students by skill level. A tiered approach, such as that utilized in Response to Intervention (RTI), identifies which students might need significant instruction in reading, those who are on or above grade level, and those who might need intermittent help (see Figure 6.1: Tiered Grouping Model). An underlying premise in RTI is that general education teachers use scientifically based (research-based) instructional practices to ensure students are receiving effective instruction. Theoretically, RTI avoids the situation where students are not achieving due to inadequate instruction. The model for RTI grouping can also be used with other academic areas or to implement school-wide positive behavioral supports. The students are then provided instruction based on their level of need. Ability grouping has also been used in math and generally is a practice in selecting athletes for A and B teams in basketball, hockey, and other sports.

Homogeneous Groups

One type of ability group is the homogeneous group. A homogeneous group consists of students who are alike. This may mean the students are similar academically. Homogeneous groups may be important to use when a difficult topic has been introduced, and intellectually, students are able to approach the task assignment in ways that demonstrate strong orientation for analysis or creativity, as compared with a concrete, sequential procedure.

Figure 6.1 Tiered Grouping Model

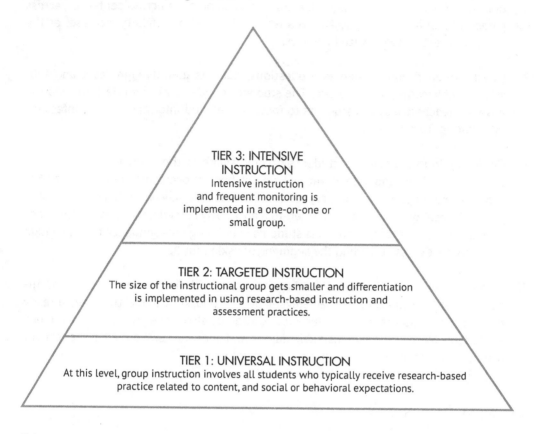

Other types of homogeneous groups may be those where students are divided by gender, by age, or by interests. Homogeneous groups often create a sense of efficacy for teachers and facilitate classroom organization.

Heterogeneous Groups

A heterogeneous group, on the other hand, is composed of a variety of students with different backgrounds. In a heterogeneous group, you would have boys and girls, different ability levels, different ages, interests, and backgrounds. Heterogeneous groups can be valuable in providing peer models for students who need to experience positive behaviors, effective and efficient methods of learning, or appropriate social skills. Heterogeneous groups may be the right choice for problem-based learning, where everyone's strengths and attributes can serve as part of the solution.

Cross-Age Groups

Designing a cross-age group may be both academically and socially oriented. Often, the academic needs of the older student are met equally, as well as those of the younger student. In some situations, a student who is one, two, or more years older will come to listen to reading or be a reader. There may be opportunity to incorporate learning games to develop turn taking or other social skills for all ages. Perhaps the older student is adept in math and is able to provide tutoring assistance. The benefits associated with achievement and confidence building for students in cross-age groups are considerable, according to Daggett (2011).

Content Groups

The type and amount of content may be the factor used in determining the type of group to use in the classroom. In a social science class, for example, teachers may have a number of themes, such as people or battles, associated with an interdisciplinary unit on the Civil War. One content group may be using maps to discover and discuss the geography and location of various battlefields. Another group may be reading nonfiction or fiction literature about the Civil War. Students will be grouped to study the selected content, but share ideas they learn with others in the classroom. Within each of the groups, the amount of content or material can be differentiated, based on learner needs.

Sometimes, content groups are organized as an exploratory studies group. Perhaps a guest speaker from a local justice agency has come in to talk about juvenile delinquency. Students may decide they want to learn more about crime scene investigation or bullying. This may prompt the arrangement of groups of students to self-select subjects associated with the speaker's topics.

Large-Group Instruction

In general, the goal of large-group instruction is that everybody learns everything. The intent of the teacher is to provide a common learning objective, common time, common materials, common instructional strategies, and common assessment. There are times when large-group instruction is necessary and appropriate. Some effective large-group instructional strategies to incorporate are as follows:

1. Carefully consider the amount of time you will designate for the large-group instruction. Limiting a mini-lesson or lecture to ten minutes is recommended.

2. Display the learner outcome on the SmartBoard, overhead, or whiteboard.

3. Give clear directions if you are incorporating an activity.

4. Circulate throughout the room.

5. Designate a time or have a routine signal to denote the end of an activity within the large-group instruction.

6. Allow time to debrief, summarize, and assess learning.

7. Incorporate humor as appropriate.

8. Adapt and use teachable moments.

9. Use your voice for drama and exaggerate gestures.

Jigsaw Groups

In Jigsaw groups, the same content is intended for all students; however, there is a large amount of text to be covered. As a result, the teacher determines the text needs to be divided to facilitate covering the topic in a more efficient manner. Student teams are responsible for a predetermined amount of material assigned by the teacher. The content of the material is shared across each group. Each piece of the puzzle fits together into the bigger picture. Using the Jigsaw approach works well for magazine, newspaper, and nonfiction texts, but not narrative text.

Connected Literature Circles

The format of connected literature circles begins with a large group presentation. Group work, using teacher-selected texts that have similar but different texts, are assigned to homogeneous groups of students. The goal is to collaboratively explore a common topic, theme, genre, author, element, or strategy. During the process, the teacher provides various levels of support to the different groups. One consideration when using connected literature circles is that it works best when multiple sets of connected texts of various levels are available for use by all learners. The texts might include high-interest, low-vocabulary reading material or text that has been modified as a result of applying the principles of universal design.

How Long Should Groups Stay Together?

In short-term groups, members change frequently. The basis for the grouping may be students' interests or needs. A teacher may quickly pair students sitting together to discuss a question. As long as the students are participating equally in the small-group activity, they may be teamed together repeatedly. As in the case of Sam, the teacher at the beginning of the chapter who used desk partners in small groups, there may be behavioral reasons or logistics that necessitate changing group arrangements.

Long-term groups may last from several months to all year. The purpose of a long-term group may be to accommodate a robust assignment with many parts that are to be accomplished over a number of integrated lessons and units. For example, a problem-based learning task may involve research, field trips and other teamwork that requires a group to invest time and build a trusting relationship in order to successfully complete the project.

What Role Do You Have in Determining Groups?

While there are times it is acceptable to let students choose groups, feedback from students supports the notion that teachers should facilitate the determination of a group, especially in the case of a long-term group project. As you plan for the use of groups, take into consideration the following items:

1. *Review the learner objectives.*

    Before implementing a cooperative grouping situation, consider the learner objective. Can the objective be met or met better by using student groups? If so, what type of group will be most relevant?

2. *Define the purpose.*

    Clearly define the purpose of the group in meeting the objective.

3. *Consider the physical space.*

    How do the desks, book shelves, computers, tables, windows, and doors impact the grouping situation in your room?

4. *Define boundaries.*

    Boundaries may be physical or academic. In short, what are the rules and procedures that will govern the group situation? Kagan (2013) uses the acronym PIES to provide structure for cooperative grouping. The letters in PIES stand for **p**ositive interdependence, **i**ndividual accountability, **e**qual participation, and **s**imultaneous interaction.

5. *Determine and locate additional materials.*

    What do you have as resources, and what will be needed? Are there content texts? Science equipment? Supporting reading resources from the Internet?

6. *Select the groups.*

    Determining what students will be in which group can be a random act, a seemingly random decision, or an intentionally determined grouping decision. Some strategies for selecting student groups are:

    • Birthdays: Months of the year often provide some similarities among students.

    • Clock buddies: Provide each student with a picture of a clock face with the hours listed. At the beginning of the week, have the students solicit a peer's name to be written on each of the hours. If there is group work that occurs during math at 10 A.M., each of the students will know who they are working with for the paired experience.

    • Color coding: Use sticky notes of many different colors or crayons to randomly assign pairs or small groups.

    • Playing cards: Dealing a deck of cards gives you hearts, spades, diamonds, and clubs, or red and black groups. These groups can be short term or long term.

"Seemingly random groups" may be necessary when there appears to be a student who is shy, less assertive, or maybe even treated differently in teaming situations. Using the color of clothing or type of shoes a student has on (e.g., tennis shoes) may be the basis of a "seemingly random group" for an activity.

7. *Teacher-determined groups* consider the need for student engagement, as well as the importance of building a safe environment where all students feel they belong. In today's diverse classrooms, there may be hesitancy to pair with certain students.

    Sociograms, where students are asked to list one or two people with whom they would like to work, may be a starting point for determining a group and building relationships between students who may not know each other so well.

8. *Student-determined groups* made up of friends also have a place for short-term group work, as choice and voice are important to 21st-century students.

What Are the Roles and Responsibilities of Students in Groups?

Group work and collaboration among students require that they be trained in the tasks they are expected to do. Below are some duties commonly associated with peer-grouping arrangements:

1. Assist: Be clear if the student is to jump in immediately and assist or wait 30 seconds. Is the assistance providing an unknown word in reading a sentence, or is the assistance helping the student sound out the word?

2. Document: Are start and finish times of the tutoring or group session to be noted? Are mistakes to be tallied or written out in their entirety? Is the peer to correct the assignment and collect it for the teacher?

3. Record: Is a narrative or summary of the action and work accomplished to be written? Is there a checklist? Or a rubric?

4. Leadership: Are tasks and deadlines to be assigned by the peer? Are motivation and facilitation part of the duties?

5. Reward: Is a token or other type of encouragement to be given? What should the encouragement sound like? How often? What and where are the rewards?

6. Assess: Is there a form to complete that provides feedback to the teacher about the success of a group meeting and individual participation?

By giving students both individual and group responsibility, some of the barriers of group work can be avoided. Several problems are listed in Table 6.2.

Table 6.2 Pitfalls of Group Work

PITFALL	DESCRIPTION OF NEGATIVE ACTIVITY
Groupthink	One person says something and everyone else agrees. No second opinions are offered.
Brainiac	One person offers to do everything because he or she fears not getting a good grade if left to someone else.
Manipulator	This person gives excuses to get out of doing work.
Avoider	An individual who doesn't respond in a timely manner or procrastinates in completing part of the project.

How Often and How Long Should Groups Be Used?

The various purposes and reasons for establishing a group will determine how often and how long a group will be needed. As the quote at the beginning of this chapter indicates, overuse of any practice can eventually reduce the effectiveness of the technique. The idea of active and engaged student learning is to maintain the novelty, while at the same time meeting the learner objective. The productivity of a group is used as a bench mark in determining the life of the group. If the goal has been met, the group's purpose has been met.

What Grouping Models Have Been Found to Be Effective with Diverse Students?

Small-group work has been found to support achievement of diverse students in classrooms. The common elements of research-based grouping models are: first, careful selection and matching of the peer participants; second, careful selection of material and content; third, training of the students; fourth, teacher monitoring and supervision.

Peer Tutoring

Peer tutoring is characterized by role taking and has been used in a variety of different settings and with different content areas. At given points during the tutoring time, one person is designated the tutor while the other is the tutee. The roles are reversed to allow the two students to be both tutor and tutee. Specific programs utilizing peer tutoring have been designed and implemented with diverse students.

Peer-Assisted Learning (and Literacy) Strategies (PALS)

Two peer-tutoring programs that are designed to supplement the primary reading curriculum are Peer-Assisted Learning Strategies and a similar program known as Peer-Assisted Literacy Strategies. According to the What Works Clearinghouse (2013), Peer-Assisted Learning Strategies (PALS) is a supplemental peer-tutoring program, in which student pairs perform a structured set of activities in reading or math (PALS Reading and PALS Math, respectively). Typically, PALS is structured as follows:

1. The teacher determines the tutoring pairs.

2. The skills presented in the tutoring session are assigned by the teacher and based on teacher judgment of student needs and abilities.

3. Peer-tutoring sessions last 30–35 minutes.

4. Students take turns acting as the tutor, coaching and correcting one another as they work through problems.

5. In reading, pairs work together three or four times per week.

6. In math, the pairs work together two times per week.

7. Tutoring pairs are changed regularly by the teacher.

The basic format of the *Peer-Assisted Literacy Strategies* is:

1. Teachers train students to use three specific learning strategies:

    a. passage reading with partners;

    b. describing the main idea (or paragraph "shrinking"); and

    c. predicting what is likely to happen next in the passage (or what PALS calls "prediction relay").

2. Students work in pairs on reading activities.

3. Students alternately take on the role of tutor and tutee.

4. Students read aloud, listen to their partner read, and provide feedback during various structured activities.

5. Reading activities are designed to improve reading accuracy, fluency, and comprehension. (Institute of Education Sciences, What Works Clearing House http://ies.ed.gov/ncee/wWc/interventionreport 2013).

Can PALS Be Used with English Learners with Learning Disabilities?

One favorable extension of PALS has been the research-based practice associated with Language Learners, according to Saenz, Fuchs, and Fuchs (2005). Once again, peer-mediated instruction is used. The process includes:

1. Students work in pairs or small groups.

2. Students are trained in three reading strategies and taught to tutor peers in:

    a. retelling (i.e., sequencing information);

    b. paragraph shrinking (i.e., generating main idea statements); and

    c. prediction relay (i.e., generating and evaluating predictions).

3. Students are taught to correct their partner's reading errors, award points for correct responses, and provide consistent encouragement and feedback.

4. Tutoring sessions last approximately 35 minutes, three to four times a week.

Peer Teaching

Peer teaching is a powerful, high-impact practice. Although there are few costs directly associated with the peer-teaching approach, it does require time to organize and set up. The premise of peer teaching is that each student is provided with meaningful opportunities to work collaboratively, establish individual and group goals based on individualized learning needs, monitor progress toward their goals, and celebrate results. Peer teaching is designed to work within the structure of the typical classroom. Differentiation is inherent, as the individual academic, social, and emotional needs of each student is taken into consideration. Various specialists, including special education teachers and ELL teachers, are included in the process to communicate with each other and document progress or suggest changes.

Referring back to the InTASC standards listed in Chapter 1, the core teaching standards align particularly well with peer teaching. As the authors of InTASC note, it is important for teachers to recognize that all students arrive at school with varying experiences, abilities, talents, and prior learning, as well as language, culture, and family and community values that are assets that can be used to promote their learning (Council of Chief State School Officers, 2011). Peer teaching promotes a more active role in learners, determining what and how they learn, interacting with peers to accomplish goals, and demonstrating their achievements.

A great deal of research has been conducted on peer teaching in the areas of reading and math. Positive impact and student achievement gains are found in both areas. In mathematics achievement, it was noted that cross-age tutors were more effective than same-age peer tutors (Daggett, 2011).

Learning Together Peer Teaching is an example of a successful differentiated instructional approach that meets the academic needs of struggling learners, while also teaching metacognition and learning strategies. Learning Together is a marketed curriculum that was developed in 1995 as Reading Together Grade Two, a one-on-one peer-teaching intervention that helped second-grade students improve fluency and comprehension. Partners in this original project were the University of North Carolina at Greensboro; Guilford County Schools, North Carolina; Hebrew University; and the National Council of Jewish Women Research Institute for Innovation in Education. It was based on *Yachad* ("together"), successfully used in Israeli schools for nearly 30 years (2013, http://learningtogether.com/company/index.html).

Cued Spelling

Cued spelling is a strategy that incorporates tutor-tutee and can also be used effectively by parents with thier children. This has been successful with students as young as seven years old. It involves both student choice and structure. Cued spelling was first described by Topping (1995) as a complement to teacher-directed instruction in spelling.

Paired Reading and Paired Writing

Similar to other peer and partner tutoring situations, specific procedures are implemented with reading and writing to support diverse learners. The fidelity of the implementation will determine the success of the student.

Duolog Reading

Duolog reading is a practice that is sometimes associated with Accelerated Reading, where a student is paired with a tutor for oral reading practice. In this case, the tutor may be a peer, an older student, or an adult, including parents, paraprofessionals, or volunteers. Procedures for correcting mistakes, discussing the material read, and assessing the student are a structured part of the practice.

Class-Wide Peer Tutoring (CWPT)

According to the Promising Practices Network (2013), Class-Wide Peer Tutoring was developed during the early 1980s at the Juniper Gardens Children's Project at the University of Kansas, a community-based program devoted to improving the developmental outcomes of children, with or without disabilities, who live in low-income areas. It is considered a proven practice that is based on reciprocal peer tutoring. Data show students learn more, learn faster, and retain more than by traditional teaching.

In brief, students are individually pretested on the week's classroom material each Monday. After pretesting, students are paired. Partners take turns tutoring each other on their spelling, math, and reading passages. They test each other's comprehension by asking questions. Each student earns two points for a correct answer and is given an opportunity to earn one point for a "corrected" answer. Each tutoring session lasts 30 minutes, Monday to Thursday. At the end of the daily tutoring session, students report their individual and team point totals to the teacher. On Friday, students are individually tested on the material presented that week.

Benefits of CWPT include successful use in kindergarten through sixth grade, general education students—as well as students with learning disabilities and cognitive impairment—have shown achievement using the method, and student achievement has been documented in reading, vocabulary, spelling, and math.

Cooperative Learning Groups

Researchers and brothers, David W. and Roger Johnson, are recognized around the world for their work related to cooperative grouping. They have identified five key elements of cooperative groups, found below:

- Positive interdependence was first coined by the Johnson brothers to mean that every member of the group depends on and is accountable to other members of the group. This interdependence serves as an incentive to help, accept help, and encourage or root for other members.

- Individual accountability supports the concept that each person in the group must be responsible to learn the material.

- Promotive interaction is defined as group members helping one another, sharing information, and clarifying explanations.

- Social skills, including skills in leadership and communication, are enhanced in cooperative groups.

- Group processing involves members assessing the effectiveness of how they are working with one another.

Informal

Ad hoc groups may be organized "on the fly" as an aid in direct teaching. Informal groups are particularly useful to supplement a lecture by dividing it into shorter segments interspersed with group activity. The advantage of ad hoc informal groups is that it will increase the amount of material retained by students, as well as their comfort working with each other (Johnson, Johnson, & Holubec, 1998).

Formal

This type of group forms the basis for most routine uses of cooperative learning. Groups are assembled for at least one class period and may stay together for several weeks working on extended projects. According to Johnson, Johnson, and Holubec (1998), these groups are where students learn and become comfortable applying the different techniques of working together cooperatively.

Cooperative Base Groups

Another type of long-term group discussed by Johnson, Johnson, and Holubec (1998) are cooperative base groups. These are stable groups that may be in place for at least a year and are made up of individuals with different abilities and perspectives. They provide a context in which students can support each other in academics, as well as in other aspects of their lives. The group members make sure everyone is completing their work and hold each other accountable for their contributions. When students in base groups meet regularly to complete cooperative learning tasks, there is the potential to provide the permanent support and caring that students need "to make academic progress and develop cognitively and socially in healthy ways" (Johnson et al., 1998, p. 10).

What Is the Teacher's Role after Groups Are Functioning?

Time invested up front in establishing the groups will be worth the effort. Anticipating, troubleshooting, organizing, and preparation will help student grouping situations run smoothly. Other roles teachers have include:

- Monitor: Once the groups are in place, check in with them to ensure the directions are understood. Monitoring can occur every ten minutes during a class session or daily, once the roles of students are understood. Regular and reoccurring conversation with each group is a preventive measure that is used to assess the status of the group process and student understanding.

- Intervention: Similar questions or difficulties may be occurring as you move from group to group during monitoring. Intervention can be as simple as asking for the attention of all groups in order to clarify the misconceptions. Intervention may be more complex if you have to address a behavioral issue with one or more members of the group. Timely intervention prevents meltdowns in groups.

- Rotate and facilitate: For some group processes, the teacher's role is more active. If you are using a Stay or Stray routine (as described in Chapter 5), for example, you will be involved in timing and interjecting the call for individuals to move to another group. You might also be rotating select individuals and facilitating problem solving in difficult group situations.

- Assess and grade: Assessment is a continuous process in groups and provides a scaffold related to academic success. Individuals and groups are also involved in the assessment of their independent work and team process and product. Providing a rubric reinforces what all team members are required to do.

- Include paraprofessionals and other specialists: In diverse classrooms, support staff or paraprofessionals and other specialists may be involved in the structure of group.

If you have a one-to-one paraprofessional, it will be necessary to determine how much or little the adult is involved in the group. Prior to organizing the student groups, a conversation to identify the roles and responsibilities of the various adults in the room could eliminate confusion.

What Are Effective Collaborative Practices in Grouping Students with Disabilities?

One process that has been used effectively when special education teachers and general education teachers team in the classroom is the Five-Step Process (2003). This applied collaboration method represents a simple, but effective, strategy for bringing general and special education teachers together to address the academic and social needs of students with disabilities in the general education setting. This process recognizes the unique roles and responsibilities, as well as the expertise that each teacher brings to the diverse classroom. Sharpe and Hawes (2003), in an NCSET Issue Brief, identify the steps as listed in Table 6.3, which was first used by the Minnesota Department of Children, Families, and Learning, Division of Special Education (2002).

Table 6.3 The Five-Step Process

STEPS	COLLABORATIVE TASK	DESCRIPTION
1	Review the standard, performance task, and curricular demands.	The collaborative general and special education team communicate about the standard and classroom expectations that the student will encounter.
2	Discuss the learning needs of the student and the availability of resources.	Teachers talk about the specific needs and concerns relevant to the placement of the student. Modifications are discussed at this stage.
3	Decide on accommodations for the student, and determine whose responsibility it is for implementing them.	The general and special education teacher creatively explore the changes that will be implemented to allow the student to more fully participate in instruction.
4	Monitor, adjust, and provide formative feedback.	This step provides an opportunity for the collaborative team to determine who will be responsible for monitoring the effectiveness of the accommodation.
5	Evaluate students using established criteria.	Teachers discuss how the student will be evaluated in relation to the target.

How Does Co-Teaching Impact Grouping and Cooperative Learning?

Models of co-teaching

One Teaches, One Observes (Assists or Drifts)

This model of co-teaching is probably the one most consistently used and misused. The one teach, one assists scenario can be implemented quickly, but often it is done so at the risk of one teacher serving in the role of an aide, rather than an equal partner in the classroom. Clearly defining roles will avoid this dilemma. For example, one of the strengths of this model is that more detailed observation of students can occur. Prior to observing, the teachers should decide what information is to be gathered and agree on a system for gathering the data. The focused observation is followed by both teachers analyzing the information as a team. There are occasions when it is helpful to conduct random checks of student activity or provide assistance to students in the room as needed. In these cases, one teacher maintains responsibility for teaching, while the other moves (drifts and assists) about the room. Sharing the teaching and observing or assisting roles reinforces professional respect and the shared decision making that is inherent in co-teaching.

Figure 6.2 One Teaches, One Observes (Assists or Drifts)

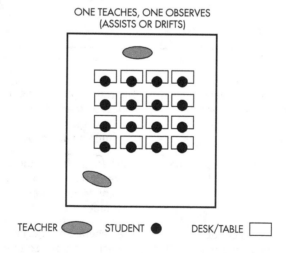

ONE TEACHES, ONE OBSERVES
(ASSISTS OR DRIFTS)

TEACHER ⬭   STUDENT ●   DESK/TABLE ▢

Station Teaching

When content can be divided into meaningful learning units and reinforced in unique ways by co-teachers, station teaching is appropriate. For example, in science there may be an opportunity to conduct an experiment with fewer students participating. Predicting and summarizing may be required at the independent station, while each of the other stations is designed for hands-on practice to determine displacement of water by different-sized objects. Teachers share responsibility for teaching content, and students rotate from one teacher to another. In most cases, because of the number of students in a class, a third station where students work independently or as pairs of students will need to be arranged. Throughout the station teaching experience, each student accesses both teachers and the independent station. One advantage of station teaching is the active engagement of students as the learner objective is reinforced and assessed.

Figure 6.3 Station Teaching

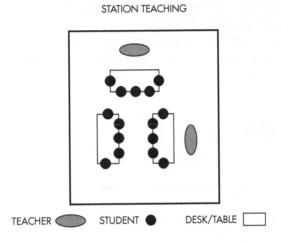

STATION TEACHING

TEACHER ⬭   STUDENT ●   DESK/TABLE ▭

Parallel Teaching

In parallel teaching, students are divided into equal groups. Co-teachers are both teaching the same information and conduct the lesson simultaneously. This may be used effectively on occasions when new or more difficult content is being presented or during a review of information. Parallel teaching provides more supervision throughout the instructional process and facilitates student learning by increasing the opportunity to respond.

Figure 6.4 Parallel Teaching

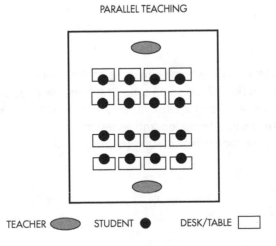

PARALLEL TEACHING

TEACHER ⬭   STUDENT ●   DESK/TABLE ▭

Alternative Teaching

In diverse classrooms, alternative teaching may be a reasonable solution to making accommodations that meet the needs of some students. Situations where a small group needs to work with one teacher, while the larger group works with the other teacher, might include teaching or reteaching math concepts, or providing multiple opportunities or more time for reading. In alternative teaching, the large group completes the planned lesson, while a smaller group either completes an alternative lesson or the same lesson taught at a different level or for a different purpose. Alternative teaching may occur during the entire class period, or it might be used for just a few minutes at the beginning or end of a lesson.

Figure 6.5 Alternative Teaching

ALTERNATIVE TEACHING

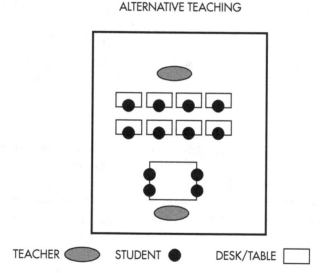

TEACHER ⬭   STUDENT ●   DESK/TABLE ▭

Team Teaching

In team teaching, both teachers are knowledgeable of the content being taught and are delivering the same instruction at the same time. Teachers speak up freely during large-group instruction and move among all the students in the class. Instruction becomes a conversation, not turn taking. Reflection and assessment of the student learning and lesson instruction become a naturally occurring by-product of the teaming.

Figure 6.6 Team Teaching

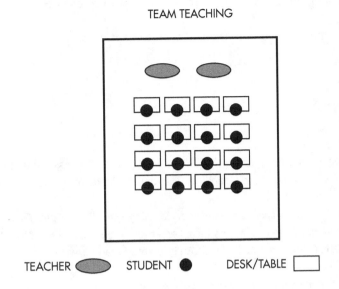

SUMMARY

Grouping plays an important role in supporting and accommodating diverse learners. Flexible grouping allows teachers to meet the needs of a variety of children. It can be used to facilitate academic success, enhance social inclusion, or promote completion of group projects. Student groups range from pairs, to small teacher-led groups, to groups that co-teachers may provide alternative lessons for during a day. Peer groups have been found to be positively related to student achievement. As with other effective practices, teachers must invest time in determining the purpose of the grouping arrangement, planning and assessing the effectiveness, and honing their classroom management skills.

REVIEW

1. Using the information provided by Sam about his classroom in the introduction, create a classroom seating and grouping model that might be used for a long-term student project.

2. Based on the six roles and responsibilities of students in groups, write a training manual addressing expectations of the peers in a grouping model that you intend to implement.

3. Be a mythbuster. Create a list of ten myths about grouping strategies (e.g., peer tutoring, social inclusion, co-teaching) you previously believed or had heard about. After you have the list created, dispute each mythical item with research.

4. Complete the templates found at the end of this chapter.

REFERENCES

Council of Chief State School Officers. (April 2011). Interstate Teacher Assessment and Support Consortium (InTASC) Model Core Teaching Standards: A Resource for State Dialogue. Washington, DC.

Daggett, W. (June 2011). *White Paper Cross-Age Peer Teaching—An Effective and Efficient Model for Supporting Success in the Classroom.* International Center for Leadership in Education. Rexford, NY.

Dickson, S. V., Chard, D. J., & Simmons, D. C. (1993). An integrated reading/writing curriculum: A focus on scaffolding. *LD Forum, 18*(4), 12–16.

Ford, M. P. (2005). *Differentiation through Flexible Grouping: Successfully Reaching All Readers.* University of Wisconsin, Oshkosh, Learning Points Associates. Naperville, IL.

Institute of Education Sciences, What Works Clearing House. (2013). Retrieved from http://ies.ed.gov/ncee/wWc/interventionreport

Johnson, D. W., Johnson, R. T., & Holubec, E. (1998). *Cooperation in the classroom.* Edina, MN: Interaction Book Company.

Kagan, S. (2013). Structures epitomize engagement. Retrieved from http://www.kaganonline.com/free_articles/dr_spencer_kagan/ASK28.php

Kaufman, R., & Wandberg, R. (2010). *Powerful practices for high-performing special educators.* Thousand Oaks, CA: Corwin Press.

Kohler, F. W., and Greenwood, C. R. (1990). Effects of collateral peer supportive behaviors within the class-wide peer tutoring program. *Journal of Applied Behavior Analysis, 23*(3), 307–322.

Palincsar, A. S. (1986). Reciprocal teaching. In *Teaching reading as thinking.* Oakbrook, IL: North Central Regional Educational Laboratory.

Promising Practices Network. (2013). http://www.promisingpractices.net/

Radencich, M. C., & McKay, L. J. (1995). *Flexible grouping for literacy in the elementary grades.* Boston: Allyn and Bacon.

Sáenz, L. M., Fuchs, L. S., & Fuchs, D. (2005). Peer-assisted learning strategies for English language learners with learning disabilities. *Exceptional Children, 71*(3), 231–247.

Sideridis, G. D., Utley, C., Greenwood, C. R., Delquadri, J., Dawson, H., Palmer, P., & Reddy, S. (1997). Class-wide peer tutoring: Effects on the spelling performance and social interactions of students with mild disabilities and their typical peers in an integrated instructional setting. *Journal of Behavioral Education, 7*(4), 435–462.

Slavin, R. E. (1991). *Student team learning: A practical guide to cooperative learning* (3rd ed.). National Education Association. Washington, DC.

Topping, K. (1995). Cued spelling: A powerful technique for parent and peer tutoring. *Reading Teacher, 48*(5), 374–383.

Topping, K., & Ehly, S. (Eds.) (1998). *Peer assisted learning.* Lawrence Erlbaum and Associates: New Jersey.

TEMPLATE 6.1: TIERED GROUPING MODEL

First, write a learner objective for a topic you will teach in your content area. Next, in each tier, identify a variety of flexible grouping options you would use to accomplish the objective. Finally, based on what you have read in other chapters, what additional differentiation practices would you use in each of the tiers to accomplish the learner outcome? Describe those differentiation practices in the boxes found next to the triangle. Each tier in the triangle corresponds with the box directly across from the tier.

Learner Objective:

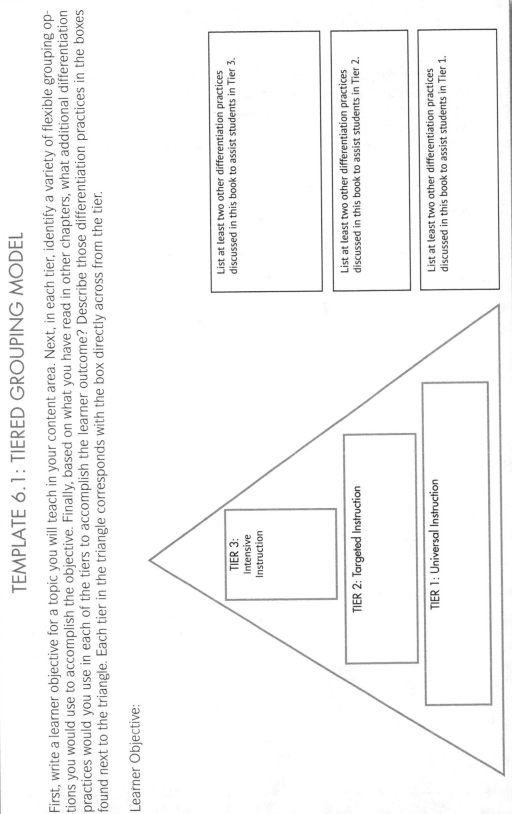

TIER 3:
Intensive
Instruction

TIER 2: Targeted Instruction

TIER 1: Universal Instruction

List at least two other differentiation practices discussed in this book to assist students in Tier 3.

List at least two other differentiation practices discussed in this book to assist students in Tier 2.

List at least two other differentiation practices discussed in this book to assist students in Tier 1.

TEMPLATE 6.2: ONE TEACHES, ONE OBSERVES (ASSISTS OR DRIFTS)

In the space below, describe an instructional situation in a specific content area where the co-teaching model of One Teaches, One Observes (Assists or Drifts) might be the model of choice. Select one of the diverse students from the case studies identified in Chapter 1. Discuss how each of the teachers would interact with the student and what advantages or disadvantages there are to this model.

Student :_____

Grade:_____Course:_____Unit:_____

TEMPLATE 6.3: STATION TEACHING

In the space below, describe an instructional situation in a specific content area where the co-teaching model of Station Teaching might be the model of choice. Select one of the diverse students from the case studies identified in Chapter 1. Discuss how each of the teachers would interact with the student and what advantages or disadvantages there are to this model.

Student :_____

Grade:_____Course:_____Unit:_____

TEMPLATE 6.4: PARALLEL TEACHING

In the space below, describe an instructional situation in a specific content area where the co-teaching model of Parallel Teaching might be the model of choice. Select one of the diverse students from the case studies identified in Chapter 1. Discuss how each of the teachers would interact with the student and what advantages or disadvantages there are to this model.

Student :_____

Grade:_____Course:_____Unit:_____

TEMPLATE 6.5: ALTERNATIVE TEACHING

In the space below, describe an instructional situation in a specific content area where the co-teaching model of Alternative Teaching might be the model of choice. Select one of the diverse students from the case studies identified in Chapter 1. Discuss how each of the teachers would interact with the student and what advantages or disadvantages there are to this model.

Student :_____

Grade:_____Course:_____Unit:_____

TEMPLATE 6.6: TEAM TEACHING

In the space below, describe an instructional situation in a specific content area where the co-teaching model of Team Teaching might be the model of choice. Select one of the diverse students from the case studies identified in Chapter 1. Discuss how each of the teachers would interact with the student and what advantages or disadvantages there are to this model.

Student :_____

Grade:_____Course:_____Unit:_____

Chapter seven
QUESTIONING TECHNIQUES

Judge a man by his questions rather than by his answers.

—VOLTAIRE

OBJECTIVES

Readers will be able to:

1. Describe how questioning strategies engage learners.

2. Identify opportunities to incorporate effective questions.

3. Create questions designed to enhance thinking and learning.

4. Utilize a variety of questioning strategies to support learning and differentiation in classroom instruction.

KEY VOCABULARY

Readers will be able to define or describe each term in the context of the chapter information:

| Big Questions | Provocative Questions | Scaffolding Questions |
| Formative Assessment | Questioning Strategies | |

INTRODUCTION

Special education teacher Juanita Myles was grooming students to use good study habits and social skills so they would be successful in all of their academic classes as they became more included in regular classroom settings. She expected her students to be honest with her, and she had also been teaching them to be self-advocates about what they needed. But Mrs. Myles noticed that every time she asked the students if they had any questions about the day's reading assignments or homework, they stared blankly at her. The dance of confusion started almost immediately. It was clear most of the students were not comprehending the content she was presenting. One student after another would confess they couldn't remember or didn't know how to complete the work. Mrs. Myles knew she should ask questions that required more than a yes-or-no response, but she was always running out of time and afraid the resource students would resist more complex questions. Why didn't they ask her questions? Juanita decided to check with Tanika Brown, her co-teacher, for some ideas on how to use questions more effectively. Ms. Brown started by asking Juanita the following five basic questions:

You can use the checklist to identity your questioning practices.

	Don't Know	Yes	No	Sometimes
1. Do you use open-ended questions?	☐	☐	☐	☐
2. Do you allow enough time for students to process and respond to a question?	☐	☐	☐	☐
3. Do you provide students with questions that stimulate ideas?	☐	☐	☐	☐
4. Do you use questions as formative assessment?	☐	☐	☐	☐
5. Do you ask questions to clarify information?	☐	☐	☐	☐

How Might Effective Questions Increase Student Engagement and Achievement?

Questions are portable. They don't require extra money, equipment, or space. A well-worded question, at just the right time, can generate an abundance of information or prompt enthusiasm in class discussion. Throughout this chapter, methods of effective questioning practices used in classrooms and types of effective questions known to increase student engagement and achievement will be identified.

What Does the Research Say?

Effective questioning requires preparation and practice. Asking better questions increases opportunity for student learning. Teachers reinforce comprehension when they ask students questions that elicit more and better responses (Chi, 2000). Scaffolding questions to ensure students are able to explore ideas beyond a surface response resonates with independent learning and critical thinking. Students, including those with lower ability, can be trained to generate explanations that increase understanding of text (McNamara, 2004; O'Reilly, Best, & McNamara, 2004). Cognitive learning strategies incorporate the use of routines that demonstrate how to ask and answer questions. Pashler, Bain, Bottge, Graesser, Koedinger, McDaniel, & Metcalfe (2007) describe the need for teachers to design effective selected-response or short-answer questions that serve as models for student responses. Students who ask and answer deep questions are provided with a richer assessment of their knowledge (Pashler et al., 2007).

As part of the lesson planning process, teachers who start with the end, or the lesson's learner objectives in mind, write questions that support formative assessment throughout the teaching activities. Teachers who focus on student learning rather than the content itself find there is a higher level of student engagement that results in increased understanding (Darling-Hammond, 2008). Big questions have become more common as problem-based learning or inquiry learning has gained prominence in education. The big question is the equivalent of the learner outcome and focuses on the big idea students are to internalize.

For students with learning disabilities, those who may have slower cognitive processing abilities or limited vocabulary, it is critical to be explicit and persistent. Meaningful inquiry is a tool that readily supports academic concepts being taught in Common Core State Standards. The ability to differentiate questions immediately by restating or reframing speaks to the versatility of questions and the responsiveness of the teacher. In addition, allowing more time for a student to construct a response reinforces a more thoughtful answer. Teachers who provide opportunity for student dialogue and reflection enhance the inquiry process.

Why Ask Questions?

Asking questions of students is a skill that can be developed. Experienced teachers use questions for a variety of reasons, such as to:

1.   Determine prior knowledge;

2.   Assess learning;

3. Clarify a vague comment;

4. Explore attitudes, values, or feelings;

5. Prompt students to see a concept from another perspective;

6. Refine a statement or idea;

7. Generate solutions;

8. Prompt students to support an assertion or interpretation;

9. Direct students to respond to one another;

10. Investigate a thought process;

11. Predict possible outcomes;

12. Connect and organize information;

13. Apply a principle or formula;

14. Provide an example to illustrate a concept;

15. Brainstorm creative ideas.

Where Do You Start?

Many teachers find that using Benjamin Bloom's Taxonomy (1956) for developing questions provides an excellent framework for their students. Since then, a former student of Bloom's, Lorin Anderson, offered some revisions to the learning taxonomy. Anderson's additions included changing the nouns to active verbs and slightly rearranging evaluation and synthesis (Anderson & Krathwohl, 2001). Examples of question stems matched to taxonomy levels are noted in Table 7.1. Knowledge appears at the bottom of the list, as it is identified as the basic or foundation level of information. As one moves up the matrix, higher levels of thinking and cognitive ability are demonstrated. Additional question prompts that support the learning of diverse students can be found in Kaufman & Wandberg (2010).

How Will You Plan Your Questions?

Most teachers are not prepared in the art of asking effective questions. You may find you have a problem with phrasing or organizing questions to scaffold student learning.

Table 7.1. The Question Matrix

BLOOM'S TAXONOMY (1956)	REVISED TERMINOLOGY (ANDERSON & KRATHWOHL, 2001)	DEFINING BEHAVIORS	EXAMPLES OF QUESTION STEMS
Evaluation	Creating	Reinventing	If we ..., how would that change ...? What might happen if ...? How could you take that and ...?
Synthesis	Evaluating	Judging	How would you rate ...? What was your reaction to ...? What was the most important idea? Would it be better to ... or ...?
Analysis	Analyzing	Examining	When would you ...? How was that like ...? How do you know that ...?
Application	Applying	Demonstrating	What happens when I ...? How can you show your understanding of ...?
Comprehension	Understanding	Discussing, Paraphrasing	Why did ...? What ideas can you add to ...? How are they alike? Different?
Knowledge	Remembering	Memorizing, Recalling Information	What is ...? Who was ...? When did ...? Where is ...?

Perhaps the student response you wanted was not forthcoming, or the question didn't elicit the level of thinking you were anticipating. Tips for planning questions include the following:

1. Establish lesson objectives based on content selected.

    Focus on important content, vocabulary, ideas, and themes, not trivial material when preparing your questions.

2. Decide the purpose for asking questions.

    The purpose will help you determine what type of questions to ask.

3. Look at the big picture.

    Start with a question that addresses a critical concept and is challenging.

4. Write main questions in advance.

    Arrange the questions in a logical sequence, such as general to specific or lower to higher level. The prepared list of questions assures that you ask questions matched to the lesson objectives.

5. Phrase your questions carefully.

    Avoid pronouns where possible. Be specific.

6. Anticipate potential student responses.

    It often helps to have another individual read and respond to the questions to reduce misunderstanding.

7. Be prepared to add, edit, or substitute additional or better questions during instruction.

    Other suggestions can be found on websites such as those provided by the Center for Teaching Excellence at the University of Illinois at Urbana-Champaign (2006).

What Types of Questions Will You Ask?

In his book, *Concept-Based Curriculum and Instruction for the Thinking Classroom*, H. L. Erickson (2007) describes three types of questions: factual, conceptual, and provocative. Factual questions are those that are easily answered with a definite response. The conceptual question is one that requires a bit more sophisticated answer, often promoting some cognitive processing and thinking. The provocative question is not easily answered. Provocative questions are designed to motivate complex and divergent thinking. Examples of each type are as follows:

Factual: What is a budget?

Conceptual: What is the purpose of establishing a budget?

Provocative: If a government entity has an annual budget, why do many nations seem to consistently be in economic crisis?

An effective teacher-questioner assists students in elaborating ideas that may be difficult to express. A younger or less confident student or a self-assured young perfectionist may presume the teacher already knows the answer and may fear being wrong, and therefore hesitates to answer teacher questions (Daniels, Beaumont, & Doolin, 2002). During a class discussion or a one-to-one conversation, there are many ways to use questions effectively as formative assessment. Questions used will depend on the lesson objective and purpose you have established. In the course of instruction, it may be necessary to use many types of questions to engage all learners. As an instructional practice, questions are critical in providing information that addresses what students are learning. Using student responses to questions informs teachers of what and how to teach. Consider the following variety of questions, as well as their advantages and disadvantages:

Yes-or-No Questions:

Examples:

> "Have you read Chapter One in your text?"
> "Did you complete your homework?"
> "Was George Washington the first president of the United States?"

Advantages:

> These questions are helpful when trying to ascertain if a student recalls information. Yes-or-no responses can be used in a nonthreatening game format such as "21 Questions" to engage students in review of content.
> They provide a quick measure of knowledge.
> You need a definitive response.

Disadvantages:

> If used too often, it may sound like an interrogation.
> Misused, yes-or-no questions can sound punitive, such as when a teacher asks, "Didn't I tell you NOT to do that?"
> Unless a visual cue such as thumbs up or thumbs down is used, some students avoid answering the yes-or-no question. This can stilt the information gained.
> A yes-or-no response only provides a snapshot, not additional information.

Information-Seeking Questions:

Examples:

> "What happens during the evaporation process?"
> "If you mix blue and red paint together, what color will you get?"
> "In this section of the poem, how is the author using metaphor?"

Advantages:

> Students are encouraged to recall and express concepts, ideas, vocabulary, and so forth.
> Teachers formulate ideas about how they taught and what information was retained.
> The information question can be used to clarify misunderstandings.

Disadvantages:

The response may take more time for students to explain.
If a clear lesson objective is not determined, too much time may be spent discussing trivial information.

Closed Questions:

Examples:

"What is the sum of 3 plus 3?"
"Who invented the electric lightbulb?"

Advantages:

Closed questions provide a definite answer.
They test students' comprehension and retention of important information.

Disadvantages:

Closed questions reduce opportunity for discussion.
A closed question increases opportunity for quick-thinking students to respond first.

Direct Questions:

Examples:

"Where did the character in our story, Matt, go fishing?"
"What are the qualifications to be the president of the United States?"
"Where did he go?"

Advantages:

A specific answer is being requested.
Direct questions can serve as a prelude to other ideas.
Guidance is provided for students to provide knowledge and insight.

Disadvantages:

A direct question is focused and typically ends opportunity for further discussion.
Direct questions that ask personal information may be considered rude.

Open Questions:

Examples:

They often begin with what, why, or how:

"How did the women's suffrage movement impact future rights for women?"
"In your opinion, what piece of technology has been most valuable to society?"

Advantages:

Open questions prompt multiple and sometimes conflicting answers.
They are effective in encouraging discussion and active learning.
An open question provides opportunity to share feelings and reflective responses.

Disadvantages:

Open questions may seem threatening to some students.
The open question may require more time.

Indirect Questions:

Examples:

"I am wondering the reason for it being so loud in our classroom."
"Do you know, how might a person get to the office?"
"Tell me your ideas." (This type of question is sometimes called a backdoor question, as it is a statement but it inquires and seeks information.)

Advantages:

Without requiring a direct response, a teacher can reframe a conversation.
Indirect questions sound polite.

Disadvantages:

An indirect question is more formal.
The message may be too subtle for some to understand.

Leading Questions:

Examples:

"Don't you agree, we should have more say in the class rules?"
"Isn't it a nice day?"

Advantages:

Leading questions attempt to persuade in a subtle, nonaggressive way.

Disadvantages:

A leading question suggests its own answer and discourages independent thinking.

Hypothetical Questions:

Examples:

> "If you found a million dollars, what would you do with it?"
> "There is only one seat left on the boat to safety, but you and one other person remain on shore. Who will get in the boat, and how will you decide?"

Advantages:

> The questions are generally nonthreatening.
> Hypothetical questions provide opportunity for creative or reflective thinking.
> These types of questions provide an avenue for brainstorming ideas.

Disadvantages:

> There may be attitudes or opinions exposed that others will disagree with or find unethical.

Rhetorical Questions:

Example:

> "What am I going to do with you?"
> "How many times do I have to tell you?"

Advantages:

> A rhetorical question may allow for some release of tension.
> The question or response may provide an opportunity to de-escalate a difficult moment.

Disadvantages:

> You may have students who answer these, and their humorous response may not be appreciated or it will disrupt the class.

Rapid-Fire, Run-On or Multiple Questions:

Example:

> "What was Amelia thinking? Why does the chicken look so funny? Do you know what she was thinking?"

Advantages:

> May provide opportunity for a teacher to narrow the focus as the questions are asked.

Disadvantages:

> Increases student confusion and frustration.
> Students are unsure which question to answer.

Questions can support or limit student learning. Teachers often think they are asking one type of question, but in reality the question or its response comes out very differently. For example, by adding the word *can* at the beginning of the question, "Can you tell me what direction the sun rises in the morning?" the response would change from direct information to a yes-or-no response. If the purpose was to gather information about the student's knowledge of directions related to the sun, you would want to ask a specific question.

What Questions Work Best for Individual or Group Instruction?

Skilled teachers are able to effectively use different types of questions with a variety of class groupings. This is particularly important when working with diverse ability groups in a classroom situation where differentiation or Response to Intervention (RTI) is implemented.

When working one on one, asking direct questions may be the most appropriate method of assessing prior knowledge or sequentially building a student's level of comprehension. Or perhaps there is a need to scaffold instruction by asking a series of questions. In pairs of students, a teacher might use the provocative questions to create good discussion between two people. The students can brainstorm and problem solve with each other in an interactive way before bringing ideas back to the large group. Teacher intervention or questioning may be more about prompting, such as, "What options did you consider?"

In small and large groups, teacher facilitation involves seeking more student responses. "What's another idea you can add to Megan's comment?" Robust large-group discussions require active listening and teacher involvement to interject just the right question in order to keep the discussion moving forward. The coordination of two teachers fielding questions is a discussion to hold prior to this method being used in a co-taught classroom.

How Do You Get More Students to Respond?

Selecting the student who will respond is another responsibility that requires premeditation. Call-outs, allowing students to answer questions without being called on, may have a place in the classroom, but such scenarios can be less efficient and reduce, rather than enhance, discussion. Students with disabilities, like their same-aged peers, may be shy or aggressive when it comes to classroom responses.

What are the instructional advantages and disadvantages of calling only on students who raise their hand in response to a teacher's question? As you think about your response, consider:

- Advantages for the teacher

- Advantages for the student

- Disadvantages for the teacher

- Disadvantages for the student

What Are Strategies for Randomizing or "Seemingly" Randomizing Student Questions?

There are times when you want the selection of a respondent to appear random, but in truth, you have considered a method to focus on a particular student or groups of students. If the day's discussion is one that a relatively quiet student can add to, notice what color clothes he is wearing. Use that bit of information to include the quiet student as a spokesperson or reporter of information. Several strategies are listed, and there are others that can be identified.

Randomizing student questions

- Drawing tongue depressors with names of student written on them.

- Using the name generator included on software

- Numbering off students at a table or in a group (such as 1 through 6) and selecting a number—all 2s will respond to the question

"Seemingly" randomizing student questions

- Students wearing a certain color of clothing

- Students with curly or blond or specific color or type of hair

- Person who was first (or last) in the room or row of desks

How Do Teacher Behaviors Engage Students during Instructional Questioning?

A positive classroom environment will encourage student engagement and responses to questions. Teachers who have built and maintain a learner-centered classroom keep the lesson objectives in mind as they consider questions about content that reinforce student learning. Table 7.2 identifies practices that may engage or hamper student learning.

Table 7.2 Teacher Questioning Behaviors

INEFFECTIVE QUESTIONING TECHNIQUES	EFFECTIVE QUESTIONING TECHNIQUES
1. Interrupt and make incorrect assumptions.	1. Listen carefully to student answers.
2. Use monotonous responses such as "good job" repeatedly.	2. Comment on or point out interesting parts of the response.
3. Embarrass students for an incorrect response.	3. Encourage students to clarify, refine, reconsider, or think more deeply about a response.
4. Fail to hold other students accountable for listening.	4. Make eye contact with the student and others in the room to promote respectful listening.
5. Respond to every comment.	5. Limit comments in order to engage other students in formulating responses.
6. Answer the question right away.	6. Use wait time. Allow 5–10 seconds for student think time.
7. Ask the same question again.	7. Rephrase the question if no student responds after 10–15 seconds.
8. "Translates" all student responses with comments such as, "I think Jim meant to say ..."	8. Summarize or clarify vague comments sparingly.
9. Call on the same student who always raises his or her hand first for every question.	9. Call on a variety of students.
10. Begin with a layered, complex question or use yes-or-no questions with no follow-up.	10. Use a sequence of questions to scaffold instruction.
11. Place less emphasis on students sharing ideas.	11. Give students credit for their responses and refer back to student comments.
12. Overuse yes-or-no questions or those requiring little thinking.	12. Follow a yes-or-no response with an additional question requiring evidence or examples.
13. Allow little opportunity or free time to ask questions.	13. Provide expectations related to asking and answering questions throughout a lesson.
14. Are unintentionally uninviting, making comments such as, "I don't see any hands, so we'll go on."	14. Create an atmosphere where thinking out loud and academic risk-taking is acceptable.

How Does Coaching Assist Students to Respond to Questions?

Students benefit from practice in learning how to ask and respond to questions. Throughout the learning process, teachers can create opportunities to build questioning skills. It follows principles similar to the Language Experience Approach (LEA). In LEA reading, the concept states that what is experienced can be written, and what is written can be read. In coaching students to respond to questions, they must have the opportunity to become familiar and comfortable with a variety of questions. Students need models in seeing questions in writing and writing questions, as well as hearing them in the classroom and responding to them. In coaching students to answer questions, a teacher provides for the variety of learners and uses differentiation based on appropriate rationale.

How Can Questions Be Differentiated for Diverse Learners in Classrooms?

Research-based practices for students who have difficulty comprehending or remembering information incorporate question-asking strategies. Graphic organizers, also classed as visual representations, are research-based strategies that have proven effective for students with learning disabilities, attention deficit hyperactivity disorder, cognitive disorders, fetal alcohol syndrome, and traumatic brain injury. The use of these strategies is also encouraged with English learners (ELs), high risk, and other struggling students. The consistency and structure of a graphic organizer, combined with a variety of questions, support learners at various levels.

By using questions to scaffold instruction, teachers model practices that students can implement as they become more independent learners. All of the practices listed below can be used with diverse learners in a classroom. Some are more aligned with factual questions, while others focus on critical or higher-order thinking.

How Do You Scaffold Questions Aligned to a Specific Learner Outcome?

If students are working on a class problem that requires them to create a small business with a realistic budget, pose a variety of questions in writing and orally for students to consider. Going back to the learner objective, you want students to use math skills—including addition, subtraction, estimating, and predicting—to stay within a proposed budget; your questions along the way might include:

Learner Objective: Based on anticipated weekly income and expenses, create a budget for your business that shows a profit.

Sample Scaffold Question #1: What kind of expenses have you had?
Sample Scaffold Question #2: What types of spending decisions did you make during the week?
Sample Scaffold Question #3: How did you determine where to spend your money?
Sample Scaffold Question #4: How realistic was your budget?
Sample Scaffold Question #5: How would you change your budget, and why?

What Are Some Strategic Questioning Techniques to Use with Diverse Learners?

Diverse learners benefit from visuals that incorporate questions. Graphic organizers are classed as visual representations (See Chapter 4) that are research-based strategies and have been proven effective for students with learning disabilities, attention deficit hyperactivity disorder, cognitive disorders, and fetal alcohol syndrome. Most of the following questioning techniques incorporate graphic organizers. Teaching students to use these supports benefits struggling students, as well as those students who are high achievers.

Learners Needing Cognitive Support

A variety of visuals can be designed by a teacher or student who needs a high level of support to find or recall information that is read. Using a written model for asking questions provides a scaffold to incorporate similar questions in discussion.

Herringbone Visual Representation

The herringbone or fish graphic organizer can be used to represent key facts about fiction literature or historic events. Herringbone organizers incorporate the hierarchy of questions from lower- to higher-level thinking using a routine method.

Figure 7.1 Herringbone

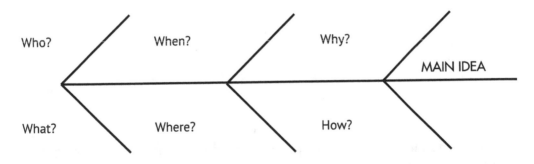

Read, Ask, Paraphrase (RAP)

Confident readers often pause to ask themselves questions and consider the material they are reading. To reinforce knowledge, students should ask questions as they read.

RAP is designed to help students with basic literal and inferential comprehension. When teachers are working with at-risk learners, the teacher needs to make sure students have basic comprehension, whether it is reading fiction or a content text. RAP is excellent for this purpose (Schumaker, Denton, & Deshler, 1984). The RAP strategy was developed as part of the Kansas Learning Strategies (KLS), now known as the Strategic Instruction Model (SIM).

Figure 7.2 RAP

Read	Read the paragraph.
Ask Two Questions:	What is the main idea? What are two details? First: Second:
Paraphrase	Put the information in your own words.

Initially, the student reads a small portion of material. Generally, this is a paragraph. After each paragraph, the students are taught to ask themselves two questions. One question is about the main idea, and the other question is about details of what was just read. The final step is to reinforce the information through a paraphrased statement. A RAP template (T7.4) is found at the end of this chapter.

Low-Literacy or Language Learners:

KWHL

The KWHL chart is an expanded version of KWL. By adding the "H," a student starts to develop a plan for independent learning and accessing resources beyond prior knowledge. Science experiments and exploring a topic more deeply for a report or speech lend themselves to using a KWHL organizer. The KWHL template (T7.5) is at the end of this chapter.

K: What do we **know**?
W: **What** do we want to find out?
H: **How** can we find out what we want to learn?
At this point, generate resources, websites, and individuals to access information.
L: What did we **learn**?

Low Motivation or At-Risk Learners:

Survey, Question, Read, Recite, Review (SQ3R)

Francis Robinson, an Ohio State University psychologist, developed SQ3R in 1941. Robinson was responsible for the Learning and Study Skills division of the Army Specialized Training Program (ASTP). The SQ3R strategy was taught to military personnel to become better readers. Using SQ3R, they were able to more quickly master the numerous fast-paced technical courses associated with the demanding ASTP curriculum (Sticht, 2002). The SQ3R template (T7.6) can be found at the end of the chapter.

The SQ3R Process

S: Survey—Skim the entire reading assignment.
Read the title, chapter introduction, boldface headings, and chapter summary. Read the first sentence of each paragraph, and scan the pictures, graphics, and tables in the chapter.
Q: Question—Ask questions of all chapter headings. Predict and look for the answers.
R: Read—Read carefully; slowly for understanding of unfamiliar information and quickly for main ideas or a general overview.
R: Recite—Answer questions you asked and participate in class discussion.
R: Review—Summarize the information you read and self-assess using ongoing review.

Figure 7.3 SQ3R Chart

ACTION	WHAT IT MEANS:
S: Survey	Skim the material. Scan the visuals.
Q: Question	Ask questions of all chapter headings.
R: Read	Read carefully.
R: Recite	Answer questions. Participate in discussion.
R: Review	Summarize information. Ask more questions.

Higher-Ability Learners:

PALBEG

Questions associated with the PALBEG strategy (Minnesota Department of Education, 2004) were originally designed to address critical reading, but may also be applied to listening. A PALBEG template (T7.7) to use in instruction is found at the end of this chapter.

Source: What is the citation for the material? Is it a credible source? How do you know it is credible?

P: Purpose—What is the purpose of this article, section of text, editorial, or speech?
A: Authority—What education, research, or experience does this author or speaker have?
L: Logic—Are the ideas logical and well supported?
B: Bias—From what point of view is this article written?
E: Evidence—What facts, incidents, reasons, examples, or statistics are used?
G: Gain—What will the author gain from this article? Will there be financial profit, votes, increased public image, or something else?

SUMMARY

Asking questions that support student learning is a skill to be developed. Setting the purpose for a question and planning the direction of a discussion by using just the right question requires practice. Big questions that challenge students to think critically readily support Common Core State Standards. Effective teachers use questions to gain the student's attention, to reinforce a previous lesson, or to encourage other student responses and reactions. Different types of questions are used to solicit knowledge or expand thinking. Engaging a variety of students to participate in answering questions involves teachers strategically planning their questions based on learner outcomes and knowing their students' needs.

REVIEW

1. Think about the courses and content you will be teaching. Develop a personal set of best questions to ask for different purposes.

2. Write a learner objective for a lesson. Create a list of three scaffolded questions from different levels of the hierarchy designed to support the learner objective(s).

3. Review the list of ineffective teacher questioning behaviors. What two behaviors will you work on to become more effective? Why are these important to you?

4. Using one of the practices under the chapter question "What are some strategic questioning techniques I can use with diverse learners?" Identify content and implement instruction for a group of students who would benefit from the routine instruction involving questions.

5. After reading this chapter, go back and respond to the five questions Tanika asked Juanita.

6. Discuss the advantages and disadvantages to teacher and student(s) for only calling on those who raise their hands. Create a list of strategies you will use to encourage responses.

REFERENCES

Anderson, L. W., & Krathwohl, D. R. (Eds.). (2001). A taxonomy for learning, teaching and assessing: A revision of Bloom's Taxonomy of educational objectives. Complete edition. New York: Longman.

Center for Teaching Excellence (2006). Effective Classroom Questioning. University of Illinois at Urbana-Champaign. Retrieved May 13, 2011, from http://cte.illinois.edu

Chi, M. T. H. (2000). Self-explaining expository texts: The dual process of generating inferences and repairing mental models. In R. Glaser (Ed.), *Advances in instructional psychology* (pp. 161–238). Mahwah, NJ: Lawrence Erlbaum Associates.

Daniels, D. H., Beaumont, L. J., & Doolin, C. A. (2002). *Understanding children: An interview and observation guide for educators.* New York: McGraw-Hill Higher Education.

Darling-Hammond, L. (Ed.). (2008). *Powerful learning: What we know about teaching for understanding.* San Francisco: Jossey-Bass.

Erickson, H. L. (2007) *Concept-based curriculum and instruction for the thinking classroom.* Thousand Oaks, CA: Corwin Press.

Kaufman, R., & Wandberg, R. (2010). *Powerful practices for high-performing special educators.* Thousand Oaks, CA: Corwin Press.

McNamara, D. S., Ozuru, Y., Best, R., & O'Reilly, T. (2007). A reading strategies framework. In D. S. McNamara (Ed.), *Reading comprehension strategies: Theory, interventions, and technologies* (pp. 465–496). Mahwah, NJ: Lawrence Erlbaum Associates.

Minnesota Department of Education (2004). Career and Technical Education Manual, PALBEG Appendix Q (pp. 50–53), retrieved May 13, 2011, from http://education.state.mn.us/mdeprod/groups/CareerTechEd/documents/Manual/007166.pdf

O'Reilly, T., Best, R., & McNamara, D. S. (2004). Self-explanation reading training: Effects for low-knowledge readers. In K. Forbus, D. Gentner, & T. Regier (Eds.), *Proceedings of the 26th annual meeting of the Cognitive Science Society* (pp. 1053–1058). Mahwah, NJ: Lawrence Erlbaum Associates.

Pashler, H., Bain, P., Bottge, B., Graesser, A., Koedinger, K., McDaniel, M., & Metcalfe, J. (2007). *Organizing instruction and study to improve student learning* (NCER 2007–2004). Washington, DC: National Center for Education Research, Institute of Education Sciences, U.S. Department of Education.

Schumaker, J. B., Denton, P. H., & Deshler, D. D. (1984). *The paraphrasing strategy.* Lawrence, KS: University of Kansas.

Sticht, T. G. (Oct./Nov. 2002). The reading formula that helped win World War II. *Reading Today, 20*(2), 18.

The Teaching Center, Washington University, St. Louis, MO, retrieved May 13, 2011, from http://teachingcenter.wustl.edu

TEMPLATE 7.1: PURPOSE OF QUESTIONS

First, identify the grade, course, and unit. Next, prioritize the types of questions from the list below to support the content objective. Behind those selected, write a question aligned with the content objective.

Grade: _____ Course: _____ Unit: _____

The content objective is: _____

_____1. Determine prior knowledge

_____2. Assess learning

_____3. Clarify a vague comment

_____4. Explore attitudes, values, or feelings

_____5. Prompt students to see a concept from another perspective

_____6. Refine a statement or idea

_____7. Generate solutions

_____8. Prompt students to support an assertion or interpretation

_____9. Direct students to respond to one another

_____10. Investigate a thought process

_____11. Predict possible outcomes

_____12. Connect and organize information

_____13. Apply a principle or formula

_____14. Provide an example to illustrate a concept

_____15. Brainstorm creative ideas

TEMPLATE 7.2: TYPES OF QUESTIONS

Write a content objective for a grade you will teach. Use the following types of questions to create a list of questions appropriate for the content. Some types of questions might be seldom used. Other questions will be helpful to scaffold learning for diverse learners.

Content Objective: _____

Grade: _____ Course: _____ Unit: _____

QUESTION TYPE	EXAMPLES OF QUESTIONS I USE
1. Yes or No	
2. Information Seeking	Scaffold #1: Scaffold #2: Scaffold #3:
3. Closed	
4. Direct	
5. Open	Scaffold #1: Scaffold #2: Scaffold #3:
6. Indirect	
7. Leading	
8. Hypothetical	
9. Rhetorical	
10. Rapid-Fire, Run-On or Multiple Questions	

TEMPLATE 7.3: HERRINGBONE

Write both a content objective and a language objective. Using a children's story you are familiar with, complete the questions in the following Herringbone chart. Identify at least five vocabulary words from the story.

Content Objective: _____

Language Objective: _____

Title of Story: _____
Grade: _____ Course: _____ Unit: _____

Herringbone (example retrieved from http://www.litsite.org/index.cfm)

Important Vocabulary:

TEMPLATE 7.4: RAP STRATEGY

Introduce the RAP strategy to a student. Select a variety of paragraphs from a text or story you would like to use in your instruction. Practice RAP consistently during the week with that student. Write the student's responses in the template. How has the use of this self-questioning strategy increased comprehension and recall of information?

Texts or Stories Read: _____

Grade: _____ Course: _____ Unit: _____

Read	Read the paragraph.

Ask Two Questions:	1. What is the main idea?
	
	2. What are two details?
	    First:
	
	    Second:

Paraphrase	Put the information in your own words.

TEMPLATE 7.5: KWHL

Using KWHL provides a model for independent learning that can be utilized to reinforce appropriate questions for students. Identify a topic of interest to you. Complete the chart below.

Grade: _____ Course: _____ Unit: _____

K: What do I know?	
W: What do I want to find out?	
H: How can I find out what I want to learn? At this point, brainstorm ideas to generate resources, including books, websites, and other individuals in order to access information.	
L: What did I learn?	

TEMPLATE 7.6: SQ3R

Select a textbook you would use with students. Complete the template below.

Grade: _____ Course: _____ Unit: _____

Textbook: _____

ACTION	WHAT IT MEANS:
S: Survey	**Skim the material. Scan the visuals.**
Q: Question	**Ask questions of all chapter headings.**
R: Read	**Read carefully.**
R: Recite	**Answer questions. Participate in discussion.**
R: Review	**Summarize information. Ask more questions.**

TEMPLATE 7.7: PALBEG: QUESTIONS TO ASK WHEN READING OR LISTENING CRITICALLY

Select a short news or journal article. Complete the template below.

Grade: _____ Course: _____ Unit: _____

Source: What is the citation for the material?
          Is it a credible source?
          How do you know it is credible?	

Identify the:	Questions to ask:
P = Purpose	Why was the article, section of text, editorial, or speech written?
A = Authority	What education, research, or experience does this author or speaker have?
L = Logic	Are the ideas logical and make sense?
B = Bias	From what point of view is this article written?
E = Evidence	What facts, incidents, reasons, examples, or statistics are used?
G = Gain	What will the author gain from this article—money, votes, publicity, other?

Chapter eight
ASSESSMENT AND GRADING

Nothing grieves a child more than to study the wrong lesson and to learn something he wasn't supposed to.

—E. C. MCKENZIE

CHAPTER OBJECTIVES

Readers will be able to:

1. Differentiate the terms "assessment" and "grading."

2. Select assessment types that align with student objectives.

3. Weight components of student tasks.

4. Describe four methods of grading.

KEY VOCABULARY

Readers will be able to define or describe each term in the context of the chapter information.

Assessment	Grading	Portfolio
Evaluation	Grading Methods	Rubric

INTRODUCTION

It has been argued over the years that many children were casualties of the curriculum, acquiring labels because they were being forced "to achieve in the artificial but clerically simpler sequence of grades, calendar and materials" that comprise the curricula (p. 209, Hargis cited in Gickling & Thompson, 1985). Current practice places the emphasis on assessing a student's knowledge and skills based on clear, consistent expectations. Achievement based on learner outcomes is the focus of instruction and assessment in 21st-century classrooms. Teachers who focus on student learning, rather than the content itself, find there is a higher level of student engagement that results in increased understanding (Darling-Hammond, 2008).

When assessment is a continual part of the teaching process, student learning is reinforced more naturally. Contextualized, relevant experiences often prove to be less threatening to students. When teachers engage with students through dialogue, the opportunity to learn grows. Students who ask and answer deep questions are provided with a richer assessment of their knowledge (Pashler, Bain, Bottge, Graesser, Koedinger, McDaniel, & Metcalfe, 2007).

Today's diverse student population sets the stage for developing a wide array of instructional and assessment practices to meet the unique academic, language, social, emotional, behavioral, and physical needs of young people in the classroom. Well-designed classroom assessment plans incorporate many opportunities to assess student learning and multiple types of assessment. Well-defined learner outcomes result in a more accurate match between teaching, learning, assessment, and grading.

This chapter provides the reader with the tools to make decisions related to assessment and grading. To understand the relationship between assessment and grading, it helps to use a medical analogy. A person who is sick often runs a temperature. A thermometer is a tool for measuring body temperature, but we often use the backside of a hand to get a quick read. The thermometer can be a digital device or a heat-sensitive strip. The temperature can be taken under the tongue, in the ear, under the arm, or on the forehead. The part of the body where the temperature is taken may yield different numbers. Some locations where a temperature is taken may be considered more accurate than others. The patient with the temperature, the person taking and interpreting the temperature, and the time of day a temperature is taken are also variables in the outcome. If there is a fever, other information is gathered to make a correct diagnosis and treat the temperature.

Like taking a temperature with different types of thermometers, assessment of student learning varies. Among other things, assessment varies by student objective, content, time of year, and intensity. Just as many factors go into making a judgment or diagnosis related to health, assessment of student learning requires prioritizing the variety of information gathered through assessment and judging it.

What Is the Difference between Assessment and Grading?

Assessments are instrumental in providing the big picture of student learning. Learner objectives, as described in Chapter 2, form the basis of accurate assessment. Selecting and preparing assessments aligned with a learner objective ensures the match between teaching and learning. Assessment is the process of collecting data by using a variety of methods. In assessment, you are gathering information about the student's learning.

Grading is the evaluative process that confirms whether or not learner objectives have been attainted. Grading is one form of evaluation. Evaluation is a professional interpretation and judgment related to the student's learning (Kaufman & Wandberg, 2010). Projects, tests, and assignments are examples of assessments that are graded. Effective decision making in assessment has several elements, including:

1. Clearly defining what is to be measured.

2. Selecting the most precise tools for the measurement.

3. Incorporating a variety of evidence-based assessment practices.

4. Prioritizing the type of assessment.

5. Establishing a degree of importance placed on what the assessment measures.

6. Interpreting the information accurately.

How Do You Know What to Assess?

What does it mean to clearly define what is to be measured? The terminology and clarity of a learner objective immediately determines the assessment. Assessments incorporate the terms used in the learner objective. Learner objective verbs include terms such as "describe," "define," "analyze," and so on (see Chapter 2). There are no surprises for students in the assessment.

The following learner objective is visually represented in Table 8.1:

After watching the video, students will be able to describe two long-term effects of a tsunami on a nation.

Table 8.1 Determining Assessment Options

LEARNER OBJECTIVE VERB →	WHAT AND HOW MUCH CONTENT →	ASSESSMENT OPTIONS
Describe	two long-term effects of a tsunami on a nation	• An essay question on the chapter test • An oral report • A science journal of natural disasters

The "learner objective verb" is <u>describe</u>. The "what and how much content" is <u>two long-term effects of a tsunami on a nation</u>. Assessment options might be:

- An essay question on the chapter test

- An oral report

- A science journal of natural disasters

Any of the options may be appropriate, but the key is, does the assessment provide you with a clear measure of how the learner objective was met? Assessing what you say you are going to assess provides a valid measurement of student learning. It is designed to measure what you want it to measure—the learner objective.

How Do You Know What Type of Assessment to Select?

The assessment you select or create and give should be appropriate. It must match the intent of the learner objective. If you want to assess a student's spelling, have the student spell. This might be oral spelling or a written test of spelling. If you want to assess a student's ability to recognize the famous works of the artist Michelangelo, you would provide pictures or replicas of statues made famous by the artist.

Selecting the Most Precise Tool

The continuum of assessment stretches from informal to formal, from observation to self-assessment, from curriculum based to norm referenced, from authentic to objective, multiple choice, true-or-false questions, and so on. In selecting an assessment, teachers consider whether an assessment is reliable. You want the assessment of the learner objective to be consistent.

Over time, the assessment provides a similar, dependable response of student learning. By implementing differentiated assessment practices, teachers are able to maintain the

Table 8.2 Assessment Continuum (Example of a Teacher's Opinion)

ASSESSMENT METHOD	STRENGTH/ADVANTAGE	WEAKNESS/DISADVANTAGE
Portfolio	Authentic representation of applying artistic methods.	Ceramic pieces are large, and we rely on pictures.
Essay Exam	Uses higher levels of thinking.	Lengthy to grade.
Checklists	Student involvement.	May be inaccurate; I still review them.
Progress Monitoring	Shows growth; computer generated.	Computers freeze.

integrity of the learner objective while meeting the needs of a learner-diverse classroom. Table 8.2 is an example of one teacher's thoughts identifying a variety of assessment practices and her opinion on the reliability of the assessment.

Now it is your turn. Using Template T8.1: Assessment Continuum found at the end of this chapter, consider the list of assessment methods and add others you use or have observed in use. Challenge yourself to consider options that may be more aligned with the goal of student learning in your classes. When finished, compare your ideas with a colleague.

There is value in using a variety of assessments that are well designed and provide a realistic measure of student learning. Teachers and students benefit from precise measures and accurate results.

Incorporating a Variety of Evidence-Based Assessment Practices

Formative assessments are an integral part of instruction. Formative assessments in a content area and grade level can be incorporated along the way to engage and inform teachers and learners. Formative assessments are defined as those assessments that provide teachers with day-to-day guidance (Black & Wiliam, 2003). Formative assessment is used to support learning rather than evaluate or judge learning. Contemporary research on formative assessment supports the depth it adds to student learning. Some examples of formative assessments used by teachers are:

- Authentic assessments—Real-life application of knowledge and skills often associated with problem-based learning or programs such as Future Problem Solving.

- Character or Case Studies—Provide opportunities to apply and discuss skills.

- Checklists—Identify steps to be completed in assignments or solving problems.

- Demonstrations—Hands-on activities that show what you know.

- Discussions—Large or small groups, sharing ideas face to face or electronically.

- Exit Cards—Submitted by students at the end of the day, such as "Muddiest Point."

- Experiments—Applying knowledge using a scientific method.

- Flash Cards—Rapid recall of facts in math, spelling, or other content areas.

- Games—Based on TV quiz shows and designed to review academic content.

- Graphic Organizers—Students design visuals of content learned.

- Journaling—Ongoing written entries related to student understanding of content.

- Mind Mapping—Quick visual schematic of what is known and connected to prior knowledge.

- Observation—Method of gathering data on students.

- Point/Counterpoint—Classroom discussions that promote seeing both sides of an issue.

- Playground Interviews—Designing math questionnaires used for graphing, percentages, counting, statistics, comparison, and so on.

- Student-Led Conferences—Scheduled discussions with the teacher to discuss status of understanding.

- Quick Writes—Briefly written responses to teacher question.

- Quizzes—End of discussion, topic, or chapter assessments.

- Self-Assessment—Critical analysis of learning provided by student.

- Service Learning—Students engage with others outside of the school to apply learning and implement a project aligned with coursework.

- Think-Pair-Share—Students are directed to discuss content.

- Think Aloud—Oral explanation of a student's method of solving a problem.

- Wheel of (Mr. or Ms.) Fortune—Creating a game to identify contributions of historical figures read about in a chapter

- Visual Representations—Pictures depicting a concept.

- 3-2-1—Three things I learned; two things I will apply; one question I still have.

What Are Some Suggestions for Using Objective Assessments Effectively?

Assessments using true or false, multiple choice, matching, short-answer completion, or essay questions may be appropriate. It depends on the learner outcome. Most objective questions require students to recall information. Written responses that are needed for essay questions provide an opportunity to use higher-order thinking skills and sometimes creativity. Designing a test with fair and equitable features is more difficult than one might think. Some helpful suggestions follow:

True or False

1. Keep the statements short.

2. Avoid using negative statements (e.g., the Statute of Liberty is not in New York City).

3. Create your own statement, rather than using sentences directly from the text.

4. Focus on important concepts, rather than irrelevant content.

Multiple Choice

1. Include the important concept in the stem of the question.

2. Each response item should be clearly stated, short, and succinct.

3. Avoid using statements such as "all of the above," "none of the above," and "A and B," which can be confusing.

Matching

1. As you create the test, structure the page with the stem on the left and each of the responses listed in a column on the right side of the page.

2. Group questions and responses into groups of seven, leaving white space between each group.

3. Label the stems with A., B., C., and so on. Label the responses with 1., 2., 3., etc.

Short-Answer Completion

1. Allow sufficient room for students to write the answer.

2. Avoid using more than one blank in a sentence.

3. Do not take sentences directly from the text.

Essay

1. When you write the question, you should have a prepared answer. This avoids the difficulty of subjectivity or trying to read something into a student's response.

2. Provide a detailed description of what is expected in the student's response.

3. Suggest the amount of time that it may take for answering each question if there is more than one essay question.

A more detailed discussion of advantages and disadvantages can be found in *Powerful Practices for High Performing Special Educators* (Kaufman & Wandberg, 2010).

As discussed in Chapter 5, actively engaging the student is not the end in itself. Active learning does not necessarily guarantee precision in assessment. On the other hand, using a scripted chapter test provided in a teacher's edition of a text may not be measuring what you want the students to learn in your class. By changing the types of assessments used in the classroom AND ensuring the assessment is matched to the learner objective, you will have a more precise measure of student learning.

Prioritizing the Type of Assessment

Not all assessments are equal. Nor are they created to assess knowledge and skills based on the learner objective in the same way. Formal, standardized assessments can be diagnostic, norm referenced, and curriculum based simultaneously. The terms are not mutually exclusive or inclusive. Over the past ten years or so, more emphasis has been placed on large-scale assessments to identify student achievement. Although such tests are used to provide a picture of student or school success, they may have limited value for day-to-day instruction.

Establishing the Degree of Importance

Once the learner objective is determined, the precise criteria for measurement can be identified and aligned with the type(s) of assessment. Providing the criteria for measurement of the outcome ensures consistency. Both the student and teacher understand the expectation. Table 8.3 below provides an example of what one teacher has determined is important.

Using Template T8.2: Matching Assessment and Criteria provided at the end of this chapter can assist you in determining a precise measure of the learner objective.

How Do I Grade Fairly and Equitably?

Now that you have identified a variety of assessment options to match learner objectives, how do you make grading decisions based on the information you have gathered? Grading diverse students in a classroom has historically created some dissension and confusion across special and general education. As content standards and expectations have become better defined, the issue of grading students becomes less problematic.

Table 8.3 Matching Assessment and Criteria (An Example)

LEARNER OBJECTIVE	IDENTIFY CRITERIA TO BE MEASURED AND GAPS	MATCHING ASSESSMENT AND CRITERIA
In written work, students will correctly use capital letters and punctuation in proper nouns and sentences.	Written work—yes Capital letters—yes Punctuation—yes Gaps: • Must there be a specific number of capital letters or punctuation types? • Does one proper noun suffice? • Must there be a specific number of sentences? • Is the content of the written product going to be included in the assessment?	Some options: • E-mail written to a business company thanking them for a product or service • Song lyrics written in celebration of a famous person or specific holiday • Business letter written to a community leader requesting a meeting • Written advertisement created to promote a new product

Taking the Myth and Mystery Out of Grading

Comics have captured the ambiguity of grades. In these quips, children tell their parents something like, "... but the teacher said F was for fun!" Or perhaps there was a time when you were asked what you got on your report card, and you responded humorously, "Grades," rather than suffer the embarrassment of scoring higher or lower than classmates.

What Is the Best Way to Design Rubrics?

Unless an assessment has a clear definition of what is to be measured, along with a precise tool for measurement and accurate interpretation, there will continue to be students who feel entitled to a grade and teachers who will engage in spirited conversations about the gifting of grades, rather than students earning them. To eliminate the reward myth often associated with grades, Quinn (2012) reinforces not only the value of clearly written rubrics, but also the need to teach students how to use them and "invite them to determine and explain their overall grade" (p. 59). When asked to grade herself, it is a rare student who extemporaneously knows how to provide an honest reflection or a critical analysis of her work. However, given a clear rubric based on standards and examples of strong, mediocre, and weak work, teachers support students in developing self-assessment skills (Quinn, 2012).

Learner outcomes are the result of standards being implemented. Regardless of content, students are required to have skills and to know and do specific academic tasks. A rubric is an instrument for organizing and interpreting criteria-driven data gathered from student assignments, tasks, observations, and performances (Kaufman & Wandberg, 2010).

Best practice confirms that rubrics clearly define the basis for how the assignment will be evaluated. Rubrics are provided to students along with the assignment.

Using the rubric provides transparency between teacher and student throughout the teaching and learning process. According to Wandberg and Rohwer (2003), a rubric should enhance instruction and facilitate learning. A quality rubric:

1. Provides students with a clear and specific goal.

2. Promotes good performance by showing quality work is achievable and expected.

3. Provides the language and dimensions for useful and informative feedback (p. 158).

Rubrics can be designed using a 3-, 4-, or 5-column approach alongside of the criteria. In a written report, students may be required to have a certain level of proficiency in areas such as organization, amount of information, and language mechanics. The components might be identified with descriptors, such as Needs Improvement, Basic, or Proficient. In some cases, a number provides a continuum of information, from 1 (low) to 4 (high). Teachers may prefer to use an odd number of column descriptors (1–5) to allow for a middle point (3). Tables 8.4: Midpoint 3-Column Rubric and 8.5: Force Field 4-Column Rubric are two examples of rubrics that teachers can use.

Remember that each box under each proficiency level must have a clear description of those criteria. For example, the "Organization" row might look something like the example in Table 8.6:

In the written report example in Table 8.4 and Table 8.5, do language mechanics have the same significance as quality of information? If you had 20 points to divide between those two criteria, how would you define the components? How would you assign the number of points? Would they be equally weighted, or does one or more have more value than others?

Teacher decisions about what is most important in learning are made every day. The value of the criteria is determined and provided to the learner prior to completing the assignment. Is the structure of writing more important than ideation? Is the experiment

Table 8.4. Midpoint 3-Column Rubric

CRITERIA	EXEMPLARY	BASIC	NEEDS IMPROVEMENT
Organization			
Amount of Information			
Quality of Information			
Information Sources			
Language Mechanics			
Diagrams and Illustrations			

Table 8.5. Force Field 4-Column Rubric

CRITERIA	PROFICIENT 4 (HIGH)	MEETS STANDARD 3	DEVELOPING 2	UNACCEPTABLE 1 (LOW)
Organization				
Amount of Information				
Quality of Information				
Information Sources				
Language Mechanics				
Diagrams and Illustrations				

Table 8.6 Sample Proficiency Descriptors

CRITERIA	PROFICIENT	MEETS STANDARD	DEVELOPING	UNACCEPTABLE
Organization	Information is very organized with well-constructed paragraphs and subheadings.	Information is organized with well-constructed paragraphs.	Information is organized, but paragraphs are not well constructed.	The information appears to be disorganized.

in science based on using the correct formula or being able to explain what failed in the experiment? The weight or value indicates the strength of the instruction given to the topic and how it is assessed.

Table 8.7: Weighted Criteria and Table 8.8: Weighted Criteria with Scores and Totals are provided as an example to illustrate one way to weight (prioritize) the criteria of the student task (assignment). Each step provides the process.

Step 1: Give your descriptors the numbers 4, 3, 2, and 1.

Step 2: Give each of your criteria a number 1 (low), 2, or 3 (high). depending on how important that criteria is in relationship to the others. No criteria should be rated 0—obviously, if it is rated 0 (totally unimportant), it should not be a criterion in the first place. In the example (Table 8.7), Quality of Information and Language Mechanics received the highest level of importance.

Table 8.7 Weighted Criteria

CRITERIA	PROFICIENT (4)	MEETS STANDARD (3)	DEVELOPING (2)	UNACCEPTABLE (1)
Organization (2)				
Amount of Information (2)				
Quality of Information (3)				
Information Sources (2)				
Language Mechanics (3)				
Diagrams and Illustrations (1)				

Table 8.8 Weighted Criteria with Scores and Totals

CRITERIA	PROFICIENT (4)	MEETS STANDARD (3)	DEVELOPING (2)	UNACCEPTABLE (1)	TOTAL
Organization (2)		X			6
Amount of Information (2)	X				8
Quality of Information (3)		X			9
Information Sources (2)			X		4
Language Mechanics (3)		X			9
Diagrams and Illustrations (1)	X				4
				Total =	40

Step 3: Assess each student's assignment by providing an X in the appropriate box.

Step 4: Multiply the importance (priority) number by the assessed proficiency number to get a total for each criterion.

Step 5: Add up the total scores for each criterion. The example has a total score of 40.

What does a score of 40 indicate? In this example, the maximum score a student could receive is 52 (assuming the student scored "Proficient" on all criteria). It's now up to the teacher to decide how to evaluate the score of 40. One common way is to use total points of all assignments; another common way is indicating a percentage, such as 77 percent (40 of 52 points).

Grading Methods

When teachers provide a rubric that matches the intent of the objective and instruction, the grade, whether given in points or percentages, will be a better match to student learning. Grading methods may pose an interesting dilemma in learner-diverse classrooms.

Interpreting the Information Accurately

How do you determine your students' final course grade? Some teachers use a percentage of the total possible points to determine a student's grade (e.g., 93–100% = A; 90–92% = A-; 88–89% = B+, etc.). Other teachers prefer to use total points to determine a student's grade (e.g., 186–200 = A; 180–185 = A-; 176–179 = B+, etc.). And some choose to use an "average" or "median" method to determine a student's grade.

Suppose four students—Belmont, Becky, Omar, and Sarah—were enrolled in the same course. Each student was administered the identical eight assessments. Their eight scores (in percentage) are indicated in Table 8.9 below.

If these four students were in your class, what final grade would you give to each of them? *Please answer this question before continuing your reading in this chapter.*

Would the students' final course grade be different, depending on the grading method? Let's look at four scenarios:

Scenario 1: The teacher used the student's "mean" (average) score to determine final grades. What would be each student's final score that would determine their grade?

Scenario 2: The teacher used the student's "median" (midpoint) score to determine final grades. What would be each student's final score that would determine their grade?

Scenario 3: The teacher used the student's "mode" (most often occurring) score to determine final grades. What would be each student's final score that would determine their grade?

Scenario 4: The teacher used a five-point scale (4–3–2–1–0) score to determine final grades. What would be each student's final score that would determine their grade?

Table 8.9 Student Assessment Scores

ASSESSMENT	BELMONT (%)	BECKY (%)	OMAR (%)	SARAH (%)
1	0	67	0	95
2	0	67	35	85
3	90	67	35	75
4	90	67	90	75
5	90	67	90	75
6	90	67	90	75
7	90	68	100	65
8	90	70	100	0
Grade				
Mean				
Median				
Mode				
4–3–2–1–0				

Which grading method do you think is best? Is one grading method fairer than the others? Which grading method would you use? Why?

Looking at the assessment scores and end product of each grading method, what analysis would you have? Are the scores a true representation of the students' learning? What would you do differently?

What would happen if each student were enrolled in the same course, but each with a different teacher? Added to that situation, what if each teacher used the same assessments—BUT a different grading method? How would the four student grades compare?

(See Table 8.10: Student Assessment Scores at the end of this chapter for a completed version of the scoring answers.)

Interpreting the information accurately suggests you have knowledge not only of the content, but of the students you are instructing. As you establish assessments for measuring the learner objective, you will also be determining the accuracy of your grading method.

How Are Grading Decisions Made?

As noted previously, teachers must make a decision how to translate a number to a letter grade. How do you determine your students' final grades? If you use a percentage to determine your grades, you will need to decide a cutoff score for A, B, C, etc. You will also decide the difference between an A, A-, B+, and so on. Will you be following a school policy that identifies the range of scores, such as 90–100% = A; 80–89% = B; 70–79% = C; 60–69% = D; and 59 or below = F?

Some teachers use the four-point scale. They will translate their scale scores to a percentage and give students a grade. Based on a four-point scale, using the example 93–100% = A, 3.72 and above would be an A. If 90–92% was determined to be an A-, 3.60 to 3.71 would be the range of scores.

To continue this process:

1.   3.0 on the four-point scale = 80–89%.

     What will be your cutoff for B+? B? B–?

2.   2.0 on the four-point scale = 70–79%.

     What will be your cutoff for C+? C? C–?

Still other teachers prefer to use total points to determine a student's grade. If a total of 200 points can be earned for a class, the points would be viewed as the equivalent of a percentage, 93–100% being an A; 90–92% =A–, etc. In which case, your calculation of .93 × 200 would determine that 186–200 points = A. That pattern of calculation would follow with: .90 × 200 = 180–185 points = A–, and so on for B+, B, B–, etc.

Eliminating Zeros

One of the controversies in grading is the use of the zero. A traditional grading system equated zero with failure, no points. In some cases, a zero can decimate a student's chance to repair and improve a grade point average.

A grading system using a five-point scale (5–4–3–2–1) eliminates the use of a zero. The five-point scale is different, in that the student's grade provides a benchmark for continued learning. In using a rubric, does the zero become less of a factor? Why or why not?

How would eliminating zeros (using a 5–4–3–2–1 scale) relate to Belmont, Becky, Omar, and Sarah in the example previously given (see Table 8.9)? Belmont received two zeros, and Omar and Sarah each received one zero. Review the scores given to each student. Discuss what you would do with the zero in each situation. What are some potential changes a teacher could implement to ensure an accurate representation of the student's learning?

SUMMARY

This chapter provides basic assessment and grading guidelines that provide teachers with strategies that offer students the greatest opportunities to achieve success. A clear distinction is made between assessments and grading. Examples are provided to reinforce the need to align assessments with learner objectives. Multiple types of assessments, from formative and informal to clearly written and weighted criteria in a rubric, are discussed as tools to gain a clear picture of student learning. Using well-constructed rubrics provides both the teacher and learner with consistent guidelines. Grading methods can be designed to provide precise and accurate measurement.

REVIEW

1. Using a graphic representation, compare the terms "assessment" and "grading."

2. Write a student objective for a class you teach, and create a list of various assessments that align with the learner objective.

3. Using Template 8.3 or 8.4, create a rubric and weight components of the student tasks for an assignment in your content area.

4. Explain how a different grading system would change the grades of the students listed in Table 8.9.

REFERENCES

Black, P., & Wiliam, D. (2003). In praise of educational research: Formative assessment. *British Educational Research Journal*, 29.

Darling-Hammond, L. (Ed.). (2008). *Powerful learning: What we know about teaching for understanding.* San Francisco: Jossey-Bass.

Gickling, E. E., & Thompson, V. P. (1985). A personal view of curriculum-based assessment. *Exceptional Children, 52*, 205–218.

Heward, W. L. (2003). *Exceptional children: An introductory survey of special education* (7th ed.). Upper Saddle River, NJ: Merrill/Prentice Hall.

Kaufman, R., & Wandberg, R. (2010). *Powerful practices for high-performing special educators.* Thousand Oaks, CA: Corwin.

Pashler, H., Bain, P., Bottge, B., Graesser, A., Koedinger, K., McDaniel, M., & Metcalfe, J. (2007). *Organizing instruction and study to improve student learning* (NCER 2007–2004). Washington, DC: National Center for Education Research, Institute of Education Sciences, U.S. Department of Education.

Quinn, T. (2012). A crash course on giving grades. *Phi Delta Kappan,* 9(4).

Wandberg, R., & Rohwer, J. (2003). *Teaching to the standards of effective practice: A guide to becoming a successful teacher.* Boston: Allyn & Bacon.

Table 8.10 Answers to Student Assessment Scores

ASSESSMENT	BELMONT (%)	BECKY (%)	OMAR (%)	SARAH (%)
1	0	67	0	95
2	0	67	35	85
3	90	67	35	75
4	90	67	90	75
5	90	67	90	75
6	90	67	90	75
7	90	68	100	65
8	90	70	100	0
Mean	67.5 = D	67.5 = D	67.5 = D	68.1 = D
Median	90 = A−	67 = D	90 = A−	75 = C
Mode	90 = A−	67 = D	90 = A−	75 = C
5–4–3–2–1	4.0 = B−	2.1 = D	3.1 = C	3.0 = C

Note: The answers to the 5–4–3–2–1 depend on the teacher's match of the percentage to the number. In the example, 90–100% = 5; 80–89% = 4; 70–79% = 3; 60–69% = 2; and <59% = 1. The others utilize the percentages given in the text examples (93–100% = A; 90–92% = A−; 88–89% = B+, etc.).

TEMPLATE 8.1: ASSESSMENT CONTINUUM

List as many methods of assessment you can think of for the students and classes you teach. Identify the strengths and weaknesses of each method listed. Use more paper, if needed.

METHODS OF ASSESSMENT	STRENGTHS	WEAKNESSES
1.		
2.		
3.		
4.		
5.		
6.		
7.		
8.		
9.		
10.		
11.		
12.		
13.		
14.		

Challenge Activity:

1. Compare your list with a colleague. Discuss why and when you would use each of the assessment methods.
2. Write a learner objective for a topic you will teach. Select a variety of assessments that allow you to differentiate while still meeting the learner objective for diverse students.

TEMPLATE 8.2: MATCHING ASSESSMENT AND CRITERIA

Clearly state the learner outcome.

List the criteria for measurement of the outcome. Providing the criteria for measurement of the outcome ensures both the student and teacher understand the expectation.

Once the learner outcome and criteria are determined, the type(s) of assessment to be used can be identified.

LEARNER OUTCOME:	WHAT ARE THE CRITERIA FOR MEASUREMENT? ARE THERE GAPS?	TYPE(S) OF ASSESSMENT

Challenge Questions:

1. Does the type or number of gaps between the learner objective and the criteria require you to rewrite the learner objective so that it is measurable?

2. Of the criteria identified, how will you use them to create a rubric?

TEMPLATE 8.3: MIDPOINT 3-COLUMN RUBRIC

Create a rubric and weight components of the student tasks for an assignment in your content area. Remember, your criteria will be different for different content areas and modalities (e.g., written versus spoken).

CRITERIA	EXEMPLARY	BASIC	NEEDS IMPROVEMENT

TEMPLATE 8.4: FORCE FIELD 4-COLUMN RUBRIC

Create a rubric and weight components of the student tasks for an assignment in your content area. Remember, your criteria will be different for different content areas and modalities (e.g., written versus spoken).

CRITERIA	PROFICIENT 4 (HIGH)	MEETS STANDARD 3	DEVELOPING 2	UNACCEPTABLE 1 (LOW)

CPSIA information can be obtained
at www.ICGtesting.com
Printed in the USA
FSHW012101040620
70878FS

9 781626 618886